Ladies and Gentlemen, EASY ACES

Also by Goodman Ace

THE BOOK OF LITTLE KNOWLEDGE
THE FINE ART OF HYPOCHONDRIA OR HOW ARE YOU?

GOODMAN ACE

Ladies
and Gentlemen,
EASY ACES

1970

DOUBLEDAY & COMPANY, INC., GARDEN CITY, NEW YORK

Greatful acknowledgment is made to the following for permission to use their material:

Three articles from the *Saturday Review:* "Growing Older Disgracefully," April 5, 1969; "L'Affaire le Butler and la Maid," May 10 and May 17, 1969; and "A Star Is Stillborn," August 30, 1969. Copyright © 1969 Saturday Review, Inc.

Manhattan Serenade, Music by Louis Alter. Copyright 1928 Robbins Music Corporation. Copyright renewal 1956 Robbins Music Corporation, New York, New York. Used by permission.

CONTENTS

PROLOGUE

It sounded so easy. All I had to do was to gather together some of the scripts of the old radio days of *Easy Aces*, and turn them over to a publisher and he would put them into a book. And as an added nostalgic touch, he would enclose in the book a brief recording of scenes from one of the programs, to demonstrate what we used to sound like.

Two walls of shelves in my den are stacked to overflowing with thousands of fifteen-minute programs which had been broadcast over the years from as far back as 1931. They had lain there speechless since the last broadcast in 1949, Jane's malaprops hushed, my reactions of "Isn't that awful?" silenced. It's only when a spring breeze riffles through the yellowed pages that I swear I can hear soft strains of our theme song "Manhattan Serenade"* wafting eerily through the room.

Well, this was going to be a cinch, I thought. But I hadn't reckoned with the co-owner of these scripts, co-owner according to an iron-clad contract drawn up by her brother, the lawyer. I explained the deal in every detail. She was quick to grasp the idea.

"What do you mean a book?" she asked.

* Composed by Louis Alter, Robbins Music Corporation, 1928.

"Just what I told you. Didn't you hear anything I said?"

"Explain it again," she said, "in words of one cylinder."

I should mention here that she suffers from an occupational hazard. Having used malaprops for so many years, she is unable to separate the original from the distorted. I tried again.

"We're going to select some of our *Easy Aces* scripts and put them in a book. It's for posterity. You'll be immortal."

"Oh, it's going to be *that* kind of a book—no sir!"

"Jane, I said immortal."

"It's all right for Jacqueline Kennedy to write a book like that but not me."

"That's Susann."

"Whoever. But not me."

"Jane, we have eighteen years of scripts, thousands of them, on those shelves. What good are they just lying there?"

"I like 'em there. They give me that good old warm, neuralgic feeling."

"I'm getting that good old arthritic feeling everytime I dust them. I don't know why you're so upset about seeing yourself between covers."

"There you go again!"

"That was an unfortunate choice of words. Listen: tell you what—you can be a co-author. Wouldn't you like to be a co-author and share in the royalties?"

"Royalties? Oh, so that's what you mean by a book for prosperity. A co-author, huh? OK, I'll pick out the scripts."

"We'll both pick them out."

"Wait, I'll get my glasses, and a pencil, and a pen, and my gloves."

"Gloves?"

"Those scripts are so dusty."

"Uh—of course. You're certainly quick to get into the mood."

"Now, dear, don't start that again!"

"I said 'mood.'"

"See that you do. OK, let's begin at the beguine."

And so we did. And this is it.

Author _____

Co-author _____

Ladies and Gentlemen, EASY ACES

JANE GETS A LOAN FOR BROTHER
PAUL

"OK, I think this script might be a good one to start with, Jane. It's about the fellow who played your brother. He was always broke. And every time I suggested he ought to go to work, he said 'Don't use four-letter words in front of my sister!' Remember?"

"Oh yes, I remember that program. That was the day I wore my new plaid dress, and that pearl necklace—or was it the cotton print?"

"That's *not* the material we're trying to select for a book. Let's read this one and see how it holds up after all these years."

MUSIC: MANHATTAN SERENADE
ACE: *Ladies and gentlemen, Easy Aces.*
MUSIC OUT

ACE: Well, first I want to say that the leading characters in this story are not fictitious. Very often, I wish to heaven we were . . . especially Jane's brother. Although Paul is allergic to work, and is the laziest guy I know, I must admit he *is* obnoxious.

Paul never shows it, but I know he hates me.

PAUL: I never show it, but I hate him.

ACE: He can't stand the sight of me.

PAUL: I can't stand the sight of him.

ACE: Behind my back he calls me names.

PAUL: Communist!

ACE: Twelve years ago Paul was in a little automobile accident. He's been collecting ten dollars a month on an insurance policy. If he ever goes to work they'll stop paying him that big ten dollar annuity. So he can't work. Paul was lucky enough to have escaped alive, and now he wants to be paid for it. Robbing St. Peter to pay Paul.

The one I really feel sorry for is Paul's wife, Arlene. They've been married ten years and she's always been destitute.

ARLENE: I've been married ten years and have always been destitute.

ACE: She never has any clothes.

ARLENE: I never have any clothes.

ACE: She's too old to go to work.

ARLENE: I never have any clothes.

ACE: How do they live? Well you've heard of people who live by their wits. Paul lives by his wits. Of course, if that's living, it's only by half. The other half Jane takes care of. Jane and I are the typical, average, married couple, living in the typical, little, Eastern town, New York City; population eight million . . . give or take one . . . And if you're going to take one, take my brother-in-law. Or for that matter, take Jane. When Jane makes up her mind to do something for Paul, she does it.

JANE: When I make up my mind to do something for Paul, I do it.

ACE: She's completely uninhibited.

JANE: I'm completely uninhabited.

ACE: And her arguments are unequivocally irrefutable.

JANE: Uh—yes, they are.

ACE: I should have suspected something the day we got married fifteen years ago. The day Paul asked if he could come along on our honeymoon. And I said no. And Jane said "Let him come along dear—he's never been on a honeymoon." And I should have suspected something the other night after dinner when Jane and I were sitting around the living room and she gave me her "Guess Who" routine. It went something like this:

FADE TO SCENE ONE

JANE: Well, dear, guess who called me up today.

ACE: Uh—Rochelle Hudson?

JANE: No.

ACE: I give up.

JANE: My brother Paul.

ACE: Oh? How much did he want this time?

JANE: Oh, he's fine. Arlene's fine too. Do you know that next week they will have been married ten years? My, how time flies. It seems like only a year ago they were married only nine years. Well, when he told me ten years you could have knocked me down with a fender. I said, Paul, you mean to say you've been married to—now just a minute

—what did you mean how much did he want? Who said anything about money?

ACE: Oh then he didn't want any money.

JANE: Who said he didn't?

ACE: Well, which is it?

JANE: Two hundred dollars.

ACE: Jane, I'm not gonna give it to him. Why doesn't the guy go to work?

JANE: Oh, now, dear, you know there are many reasons.

ACE: I'd like to hear 'em.

JANE: Well, the third reason is because—he always—

ACE: Wait a minute—what happened to win and place?

JANE: Beg pardon?

ACE: What are the first two reasons?

JANE: First because he was sick last year. You know: he was just about to get a job when he got intentional flu.

ACE: I knew you'd finally come up with the right word.

JANE: And besides, like Paul says—what's the dollar worth today? Practically nothing.

ACE: Oh, so he's not going to work until the dollar gets back to what it should be worth?

JANE: Yes, fifty-seven cents.

ACE: Of course.

JANE: Well, we talked it over, and Paul decided to come to your office tomorrow morning, I told him.

ACE: Jane, I haven't *got* two hundred bucks to throw away.

JANE: Are you insinuating that my brother isn't going to pay you back?

ACE: Oh no, of course not. He's as good as gone—gold.

MUSIC BRIDGE

ACE: As usual, as in any argument with Jane about her brother, I ran second and paid two-eighty to place. Because the next morning when I got to my office—oh, I oughta tell you this—I work in the advertising business —make a nice living—minus withholding and social security. It's a pretty fair job—of course Jane always exaggerates my importance there by telling everybody I'm a big cog in the machinery.

JANE: He's a big clog in the machinery.

ACE: The only thing I can't stand about the job is my secretary—Miss Anderson. Why don't I get rid of her? She's a cousin of Jane's twice removed. That is, I removed her twice but Jane got her job back three times. With the score now three to two in her favor, Miss Anderson practically runs the office her way.

ANDERSON: I practically run the office my way.

ACE: Oh she's a doll. D-U-L-L. So I got to my outer office about nine-thirty the next morning and I asked Miss Anderson if there had been any calls.

ANDERSON: Yes, Joe Davis called.

ACE: Joe Davis? Who's he? What did he want?

ANDERSON: He wanted a date for Saturday night. I told him I

was going to the movies Saturday night with Bill Wilson; so I gave him Wednesday night, we're going dancing. Joe's an awfully good dancer—much better than Bill—

ACE: Miss Anderson, were there any side line calls? I mean for *me*—the advertising business?

ANDERSON: Let me see—there was somebody—who was it now?

ACE: Isn't that awful? (FOOTSTEPS) if the thought comes to you, Miss Anderson, you'll be in touch with me. I'll just go into my office and wait.

ANDERSON: Oh sure, I'll let you know if it comes to me.

DOOR OPENS INTO OFFICE

PAUL: Well there you are. Is that a nice thing to do—keep your brother-in-law waiting?

ACE: Miss Anderson—is this the uh—

ANDERSON: Oh yes, that's it. Your brother-in-law is waiting in your office to see you.

ACE: Miss Anderson take a letter.

ANDERSON: A letter?

ACE: To China—and don't hurry back.

DOOR CLOSES

PAUL: Well, brother, how's the world treating you?

ACE: Not very often.

PAUL: I haven't seen you in some time . . . how long has it been?

ACE: About twenty-five dollars ago. Paul, would you *mind* taking your overcoat off my desk?

PAUL: Oh sure, excuse me. Recognize the overcoat?

ACE: Yes. I recognize it.

PAUL: You gave it to me two winters ago, remember? Lucky we're the same size.

ACE: I was born lucky . . . Look Paul, Jane tells me you want me to give you two hundred dollars. Is that right?

PAUL: Not give—lend. Watch your language.

ACE: Sue me . . . the answer is *no!*

PAUL: Oh now wait a minute, brother—it isn't for myself I want the two hundred. It's for Arlene. We have a tenth wedding anniversary next Wednesday. And I want to get her something she needs pretty bad.

ACE: For two hundred dollars.

PAUL: Yes.

ACE: Like what?

PAUL: I'm getting her a tonsillectomy.

ACE: You're going to have your wife's tonsils removed as an anniversary present?

PAUL: Why not? It's something practical.

ACE: Hm—something she wouldn't buy for herself.

PAUL: Yeh, that's it. How about it—let me have two hundred?

ACE: No.

PAUL: Well, could you make it one hundred?

ACE: Gonna have one of her tonsils out?

PAUL: Yeh. No. I could pay a hundred down—

ACE: And get the rest from me later. Nothing doing. I can't afford it. It's not the principle, it's the money.

PAUL: But I'm gonna pay you back. I keep track of every cent you—

ACE: I'm sorry, Paul. And look, kid, if you have to come to my office, and sit around with your feet scratching up my desk, I wish you wouldn't be wearing my shoes.

MUSIC BRIDGE . . . TO SCENE TWO

ACE: With my *no* ringing in his ears, and my overcoat hanging on his back, Paul walked directly from my office, to my home, in my shoes, to see my wife. Before we look in on this tender little scene, I ought to tell you that, like the typical, average family, we live next door to a radio announcer. Fellow named Ken Roberts. Ken is the only celebrity Jane knows and every time he comes to the house, which is about once a day, Jane gets his autograph. Ken loves it. So before Paul got to the house, Ken was visiting with Jane.

KEN: Hey, Jane, that's an attractive dress you're wearing today.

JANE: You do? . . . Thanks, and may I return the compliment and say it's one of my favorites, too. Where've you been, Ken, long face no see.

PAUL: Jane, are you home?

DOOR CLOSES

JANE: Oh, it's my brother. Yes, Paul—here we are in here. Hello, Paul.

PAUL: Sis, I was just over talking to that husband of yours.

JANE: Just fine—Oh you remember Ken Roberts, don't you, Paul?

PAUL: Oh, sure. Hi, Ken . . . Well, Janie, he turned me down. My own brother-in-law wouldn't lend me two hundred dollars. I've *gotta* have that money, Jane, and you've gotta help me.

JANE: Paul, you know I'd give you my bottom shirt, but I haven't got two hundred dollars.

PAUL: What kind of a town is this? Isn't there any place a fellow can borrow two hundred dollars?

KEN: This may be an idea. One of the commercials I do is "Friends, do you need money? Come to the Confidential Loan Company. You can borrow up to three hundred dollars on one signature alone. Every transaction is treated most confidentially." Why don't you go down there and borrow the money?

PAUL: The Confidential Loan Company—yes, I never thought of that. How about it, sis, will you sign my note for me?

JANE: Oh, sure, Paul. I'll go down to the loan company with you. I'll be ready in a jitney.

MUSIC BRIDGE . . . FADES TO SCENE THREE

ACE: So Jane and her brother Paul decided to go to the Confidential Loan Company to borrow two hundred dollars. All this I didn't know. But as the crime was reconstructed for me later, Jane and her brother arrived at the loan company, and Jane, as usual, took charge.

JANE: How do you do. I'm Mrs. Ace.

WILKERSON: How do you do, and what may I do for you, madame?

JANE: We'd like to see some money, please.

WILKERSON: I beg your pardon?

JANE: We'd like to see some of that money you advertise to lend. What is your name?

WILKERSON: *See* some?

JANE: How do you do, Mr. Seesome.

WILKERSON: How do you do.

JANE: This is my brother, Paul Sherwood—this is Mr. Seesome, Paul.

PAUL: How do you do, Mr. Seesome.

WILKERSON: No, I'm Mr. Wilkerson.

JANE: You said Seesome.

WILKERSON: No, *you* said Seesome.

JANE: No, Mr. Seesome, I said what is your name?

WILKERSON: My name is Wilkerson.

JANE: How do you do, I'm still Mrs. Ace.

WILKERSON: How do you do.

JANE: And this is my brother, Paul Sherwood, still.

WILKERSON: How do you do, Mr. Still . . . Now madame, did you say you want to borrow some money?

JANE: *Please*, Mr. Seesome, not so loud. It says confidential. Are you the confidence man I have to see?

WILKERSON: I'm Mr. Wilkerson in charge of loans. Have chairs, please. (SOUND OF CHAIRS)

JANE: Thank you. Sit down, Paul.

WILKERSON: Is this your first loan with our company, Mrs. Ace?

JANE: Yes, it is. Why? Your advertisement doesn't say experience necessary.

WILKERSON: No, I mean, have you an established credit here? What is your full name please?

JANE: Jane Ace. Mrs. Jane Ace.

WILKERSON: Mrs. Jane Ace—

JANE: How do you do.

WILKERSON: How do you do, I'm Mr. Wilkerson.

JANE: Yes, we've met. And this is my brother Paul Sherwood.

PAUL: How do you do, Mr. Seesome.

WILKERSON: I've *met* your brother and my name isn't Seesome, it's Wilkerson! Now how much money do you want to borrow, Mrs. Ace?

JANE: Please, Mr. Wilkerson, if you're gonna keep talking that loud I'd rather see Mr. Seesome.

WILKERSON: There is no Mr. Seesome. I lend the money. Now how much do you want?

JANE: Two hundred and twelve dollars and seventy-five cents.

WILKERSON: Two hundred and twelve seventy-five—that's rather an odd amount, isn't it?

PAUL: Well the two hundred is for me. I'm getting my wife a tonsillectomy for an anniversary gift.

JANE: Yes, and on the way down I saw a sale on hats for twelve seventy-five, so I thought we might as well kill two birds with one loan, you see? . . . Well, Mr. Wilkerson?

WILKERSON: Uh—just a minute. You, sir—you're getting your wife a tonsillectomy as an anniversary gift?

PAUL: That's right. I'm not working right now and this money will come in pretty handy.

JANE: And I'm gonna sign the note for him.

WILKERSON: I see. He isn't working—and you—and what is *your* business, Mrs. Ace?

JANE: Sister to the defendant.

WILKERSON: What's that?

JANE: I'm his sister. But I haven't got any money to lend him.

WILKERSON: Then what good is your signature on a note?

JANE: What good? Well I don't know who *would* sign for a person if his own *sister* wouldn't, and if I'm wrong I'm not far from it.

WILKERSON: You're what?

JANE: Doesn't it to you?

WILKERSON: (QUIETLY TRYING TO COLLECT HIS WITS) Uh—let me see what happened. I was sitting here in my office, quietly reading Dick Tracy when she came in and said he wanted to borrow two hundred and twelve dollars and seventy-five cents. And she wants to sign the note, and she has no security. (UP NOW) Do you have any charge accounts in any of the stores, Mrs. Ace?

JANE: Oh sure. But I wouldn't want them to know about borrowing this money.

WILKERSON: Just a minute. I'll call upstairs and check on your credit. (BUZZ AND CLICK)

MARTIN: (LOUDSPEAKER) Yes? Martin speaking. Over.

WILKERSON: Martin, this is Wilkerson. I have a Mrs. Jane Ace here who wants to borrow two hundred and twelve dollars and seventy-five cents. Will you check her credit for me?

MARTIN: (LOUDSPEAKER) Mrs. Jane Ace wants to borrow two hundred and twelve dollars and seventy-five cents? Over.

JANE: Fine confidential.

WILKERSON: That's right, Martin. Two twelve seventy-five.

MARTIN: That's a rather odd amount, isn't it? Over.

WILKERSON: Well two hundred is for a tonsillectomy her brother is giving his wife for a wedding anniversary.

MARTIN: Testing, one-two. Testing, one-two. Sounded like you said he's giving her a tonsillectomy for a wedding anniversary. Over.

WILKERSON: That's right, Martin. And the other twelve seventy-five is for a hat she saw in a clearance sale on the way down here. *Check* it, will you, Martin?

MARTIN: Will do.

WILKERSON: Roger. (CLICK)

JANE: Mr. Wilkerson, was that coast to coast?

WILKERSON: What? Oh, that's our efficient credit system. It'll only take a minute. And while we're waiting you can look

over this application. Here are the weekly rates—for a
loan of two hundred and twelve seventy-five, you'll have
to pay back four dollars and forty cents a week for one
year.

PAUL: Four dollars and forty cents a week? That's reasonable. (BUZZ)

WILKERSON: There's Martin again.

JANE: This must be the repeat broadcast for the West Coast.
(CLICK)

WILKERSON: Yes, Martin?

MARTIN: (LOUDSPEAKER) Mrs. Ace is NG. All charge accounts
are in her husband's name. He's OK. Over.

WILKERSON: Roger. Thanks, Martin. (CLICK) Sorry Mrs. Ace,
you're NG.

JANE: What's that mean? Not guilty?

WILKERSON: Yes—no! It means your signature is not acceptable.
But if your husband will sign this note, we'll make the
loan. Take that application and have him sign it.

JANE: Well, OK, I guess we'll have to do it, Paul.

PAUL: But he'll never sign that note, Jane.

JANE: Just leave it to your Uncle Dulcy. We'll see you later,
Mr. Seesome . . .

MUSIC BRIDGE . . . FADE TO SCENE FOUR

ACE: As Jane and Paul sailed out of the Confidential Loan
Company, they waved a fond farewell to Mr. Wilkerson
sinking slowly in the west. If you were a betting man
wouldn't you give a hundred to one I wouldn't sign that

note? Save your money. A few minutes before Jane and her brother got to my office, I had a visit from my boss—that would be Mr. J. K. Norris—of Dutton, Sutton, Mutton and Norris . . . I don't know how *he* got in there. Mr. Norris talks like a copy book. He believes a man's best friend is his motto:

NORRIS: Don't put off till tomorrow, what you can do today.

ACE: He's been married three times.

NORRIS: If at first you don't succeed, try, try again.

ACE: But in spite of his corny talk I like J.K. He's a lonely man—has no children.

NORRIS: If at first you don't succeed—

ACE: Yes. As I was saying, just before Jane and Paul got to my office, Mr. Norris had come rushing in quite pleased with an advertising idea I had thought up for a new account we were going to handle.

NORRIS: Mr. Ace, my congratulations on that advertising campaign for our new account, the Confidential Loan Company.

ACE: Well, thank you, Mr. Norris.

NORRIS: I knew when you and Thomson got together you'd turn out a great campaign. Two heads are better than one, I always say.

ACE: But I did this one myself, Mr. Norris.

NORRIS: Yourself? Good work, Mr. Ace. Too many cooks spoil the broth, I always say.

ACE: Yes, you do—

NORRIS: By the way the Confidential loan people are very

concerned about the type of man we're assigning to their account; they want to be sure you've never signed a note over there on a loan—or borrowed money—

ACE: Oh no, I never—

NORRIS: Good. Neither a borrower nor a lender be, I always say. We had one man here who borrowed money from them—speculated in the stock market—you're not speculating, are you? I heard a rumor you were.

ACE: It's not true.

NORRIS: That's good. A fool and his money are soon parted, I always say.

DOOR OPENS

JANE: Hello, dear.

ACE: Oh hello Jane, I always say.

JANE: Hello, Mr. Norris.

NORRIS: You're just in time, Mrs. Ace.

JANE: Just fine. This is my brother, Paul, Mr. Norris.

NORRIS: How do you do.

PAUL: Glad to meet you, Mr. Norris.

NORRIS: Mrs. Ace, I was just congratulating your husband on a fine job he did on one of our accounts.

ACE: Oh it was nothing really, Mr. Norris—

NORRIS: Nothing, he says. Don't let his modesty fool you, Mrs. Ace.

JANE: All right.

NORRIS: I hope you're as proud of him as I am.

JANE: Oh you are.

NORRIS: Congratulations again, Mr. Ace. This campaign will make you famous in advertising circles. How about it, Mrs. Ace—your husband's a celebrity.

ACE: (MODESTLY) Oh now, please.

JANE: A celebrity. Dear, I'm so proud of you. It's like having a movie star in the family.

ACE: Movie star—I suppose you'll be asking for my autograph.

JANE: Autograph? Yes—that's an idea—give me your autograph, dear.

ACE: Oh, now that's carrying a joke too—

JANE: But dear, you're a celebrity—

ACE: I know, but—

NORRIS: Go ahead, Mr. Ace—give your wife your autograph.

ACE: But, Mr. Norris—it's embarrassing . . .

JANE: Here you are dear—on this piece of paper—right here —here's your pen—

ACE: I feel kinda idiotic—what is this paper I'm—

NORRIS: Go ahead, sign your name—

ACE: Haha all right—here you are— (SOUND OF PEN) Haha this is kinda silly—autograph to my own wi—

JANE: That's it—thanks, dear. Gimme that. (SOUND OF PAPER)

PAUL: Nice work, sis.

ACE: What is that paper you gave me to—

NORRIS: Well, Mrs. Ace, let's clear out and leave the big man to his own thoughts. Confidentially I think he wants to be alone.

JANE: Yes—that's exactly where *I'm* going. Come on Paul— see you later, dear.

MUSIC BRIDGE . . . TO SCENE FIVE

ACE: All I can say in defense of my simpering self, is that I have a good alibi . . . I'm stupid. And I never would have known I even signed the thing, if something hadn't happened a week later. Jane and I were sitting around the living room after dinner and I was doing a little bragging: "Jane, remember that advertising cámpaign Mr. Norris congratulated me on about a week ago? He gave me a five-hundred-dollar bonus today. Pretty good, huh?

JANE: Yes, dear.

ACE: Is that the most enthusiasm you can work up? I thought at least you'd cheer.

JANE: Yippee, dear.

ACE: Well, *thanks*, if you can spare that. Maybe this'll brighten you up. I'm going to take two hundred of this bonus and lend it to Paul. Arlene does have to have her tonsils out and as long as I—

JANE: Paul got that money already.

ACE: Where?

JANE: Last week. But I'll tell you what you can do.

ACE: I said where did Paul get that—

JANE: If you want to do somebody a favor, how about increasing my allowance?

ACE: Where did Paul get the two hu—increase your allowance? How much?

JANE: Four dollars and forty cents a week.

ACE: Four forty—how'd you arrive at that round figure?

JANE: Well I might as well get this off my chin.

ACE: OK, start chinning.

JANE: I'll make it short and sappy. Remember last week when I came to your office and you were a celebrity and you signed your autograph on a piece of paper I gave you?

ACE: Fine celebrity. Yes?

JANE: Well, that day you opened a charge account at the Confidential Loan Company.

ACE: Confiden—oh no.

JANE: Paul borrowed two hundred dollars when you autographed the note.

ACE: No!

JANE: That's the price of fame, dear.

ACE: Oh no!

JANE: Oh yes. And today they called up that Paul missed the first payment. Four dollars and forty cents.

ACE: And he's gonna miss every other payment, and I'm gonna have to make it good.

JANE: I should say you won't. What kind of a wife do you think I am? I got you into this and I'm gonna make it good myself. I'll pay it out of my allowance. All you have to do is raise my allowance four forty a week.

ACE: Look, Ponzi, I don't even mind the money now. But

when the Confidential Loan Company finds out I signed
that note they'll cancel their advertising account.

JANE: No they won't, dear. When he saw your signature he
asked me if you're in the advertising business and I said
yes, and he laughed and said he was glad to have somebody like you handling their advertising.

ACE: Laughed? Glad?

JANE: He said he only wished all the other signers they have
would be as happy to sign a note as you were?

ACE: Who told him I was happy?

JANE: He could tell the way you signed it. He said this was
the first time in his experience that a co-signer ever signed
a note: "Sincerely yours, with all my love."

ACE: Isn't that awful?

MUSIC PLAY OFF

JANE SERVES ON A JURY

ACE: That script ought to be OK. Of course I don't think you can get a tonsillectomy these days for only two hundred dollars.

JANE: That's because in those days they didn't have those cutthroat prices.

ACE: I knew you'd stumble on the right word one day. Oh, before I forget, I should tell you they're going to use photographs of us in this book.

JANE: Oh, it's going to be a book with pictures? Good. Saves reading.

ACE: No, the pictures will be on the front and back covers. We have a lot of them lying around back there.

JANE: Yes, and I'd like to use my favorite picture—the one I was going to use when I thought of going on the stage and being a big Broadway star but you wouldn't let me. I'll go get it. I'll be back in a jitney.

While she's gone, I should fill you in on that stage bit. That was in the early days of radio when success went to Jane's head, where it had plenty of room to bounce around. As I recall it, it went something like this:

"What do you think about my going on the stage?" she asked.

"As what?" I inquired.

"As a star," she replied. "I can become famous and rich."

"Oh, not that routine again."

"Yes you will."

"Look, Jane, let's face facts. You've never been on the stage, you can't read lines, you don't know how to project, and above all you have no talent to become a famous star and rich. Now do you understand how I feel about you and a stage career?"

"Yes. You're afraid that when I become famous and rich, I'll divorce you."

"Promises, promises."

"OK, I promise I won't, even if I become a big dramatic star, or even in musical comedy, because my friends say I sing like an angel."

"Sure, like an angel. But can't you wait till you get up there?"

"I've waited too long already, just laying around the house."

"That's 'lying.'"

"No, it's the truth."

"Jane, listen, what qualifications do you have to become an actress?"

"Not much, I haven't. I've always had the smell of goose grease in my blood. I've always dreamed of seeing my name up in tights."

"OK, Gypsy, I give up. You're going to be another Sarah Bernhardt."

"Or bigger. Of course I'm going to start small. I play a maid in this play. That's what I've been trying to tell you if you'll stop shouting yourself hoarse in the face."

"Whoa, back up. What play is that?"

"It's a play our club is putting on. The W-O-M-A-N."

"What's that stand for?"

"Woman."

"Oh, of course, how stupid of me."

"I forgive you, dear. In this play I'm the maid, and I have one line. I come in and I say to Mable—she plays the leading part—I say, 'Your coat, madame.' That's the one line I have."

"And from that you expect to be discovered?"

"What discovered! I'm already here. They'll see me when I say 'Your coat, madame' and I hold it while she puts it on and I walk off, and when the audience applauds I take a bow."

"Applause for holding a coat?"

"Well, you're going to be in the audience. You can start it. You know how people are. Don't they always yawn when somebody else yawns? And so can you."

"Yes, I can do that all right."

"Thank you, dear. And don't you worry about the divorce. I wouldn't ever leave you."

"Why not?"

"You're welcome. Now, there's one problem. Well it's not exactly a problem, because I can always use it."

"How's that again, I'm afraid to ask?"

"Well, we each have to bring our own costumes. So I want to look my best, and my best would be in a mink coat."

"A maid wearing a mink coat?"

"No, I don't wear it. The coat I hold up for Mable."

"You're kidding."

"You don't expect me to hold up my three-year-old Persian lamb, do you? To say nothing of my raincoat."

"Jane, if your stage career depends on a mink coat, forget it."

"Forget the stage? Why any girl would give her right name

to become a star. And I'm going to be on Broadway or my name is Maude. Where are you going?"

"I'm going to buy two tickets and applaud you on opening night, Maude."

"Oh, thank you, dear. Two tickets? Who are you going with? I see—when the cat's on the stage the mouse will play."

And so on. Although she had hitched her wagon to a star, Jane finally settled for a microphone—thank heaven. As for the mink coat, you know how that was solved?

Since I was adamant about it, Jane suggested to the play committee that the first act be played with thunder and lightning offstage to simulate a rainstorm. Mary Babs Moore, eminent electrician of all the WOMAN plays, naturally loved the idea. So the coat that was held up for madame was Jane's raincoat.

ACE: Well that's the way it was. Now to the next script.

MUSIC IN: MANHATTAN SERENADE
ACE: *Ladies and gentlemen, Easy Aces.*
MUSIC OUT

ACE: The Constitution of the United States says that every man is entitled to a trial by a jury of his peers . . . Peers . . . Funk and Wagnalls, in their latest best seller entitled Dictionary, have this definition of Peer.

WAGNALLS: A peer is a person of equal intellect, knowledge, understanding, and intelligence.

ACE: Thank you, Mr. Funk.

WAGNALLS: I'm Wagnalls.

ACE: Oh, sorry . . . Equal intellect—intelligence. Now with

that definition in mind, it becomes quite obvious they selected Jane, alphabetically. But don't get the wrong idea: as a housewife, Jane has no equal. She's a human dynamo.

JANE: As a housewife, I have no equal. I'm a human domino.

ACE: I should know, after all she is my lawful wedded wife.

JANE: He should know. After all I am his awful wedded wife.

ACE: But she's never even seen the inside of a courtroom.

JANE: I saw the movie *The Paradine Case* three times.

ACE: The summons for jury duty arrived as we were having breakfast, and Jane of course was quite excited about it.

JANE: But dear, I didn't do it. I'm not guilty. I've got an alibi. Who saw me? I only hit the gum machine once—nothing came out—I couldn't get my penny back.

ACE: Gum machine—what are you talk—

JANE: How long can they give me—will you come up to visit me?

ACE: Jane, will you stop—this is only a summons to serve on a jury—somebody else is on trial. Not you.

JANE: You sure? This has nothing to do with—

ACE: Oh sit down, and stop worrying. Fine juror you're gonna make.

JANE: How did they happen to think of me? I never jured before. What do I have to do?

ACE: All you have to do is sit in a jury box and listen to the evidence. It says a petit jury—that's a civil case, somebody probably suing somebody for money, and you have to decide whether he gets the money or not. And oh yes, a juror gets paid three dollars a day.

JANE: I do? Oh well, then I'll say he's not guilty.

ACE: Who's not guilty?

JANE: Well, whoever it is—after all if he's nice enough to pay me three dollars a day to be his jury, the least I can do is recuperate and say he didn't break the gum machine, doesn't it to you?

ACE: Jane, you don't even know what the case is about. You can't make up your mind in advance—you have to be unbiased.

JANE: Un-what?

ACE: Unbiased. Means you gotta have an open mind.

JANE: Oh well, I've got an open mind.

ACE: Yes, they needed you like a hole in a head. (DOOR BUZZ)

JANE: That must be Paul.

ACE: I need him that way too.

JANE: I'll let him in dear . . .

ACE: While Jane goes to let in her brother Paul Sherwood, I oughta tell you something about him. Paul is now in the construction business. Right now he's overseeing a big project at 45th and First Avenue, the new United Nations Building. His office is the third peephole from the left overlooking the steam shovel. Another thing he overlooks is getting a job. He thinks working for a living is for peasants. He hopes to make his fortune with one stroke of genius. He spends most of his time playing cards.

PAUL: I spend most of my time playing cards.

ACE: That's why he's never reached the pinnacle of success.

PAUL: I'm a success at pinochle.

ACE: OK, now you've met him, you can have him. Jane's opening the door to let him in. (DOOR OPENS)

PAUL: Good morning, sis. How are you? (DOOR CLOSES)

JANE: Paul, the most exciting thing. I just got a summons for —oh, I'm fine.

PAUL: Hiya brother. Don't get up.

ACE: Who's getting up?

PAUL: I just happened to be passing on my way down to—

ACE: Oh no—not that same routine again—Paul we know you always happen to be passing at breakfast time. Just sit down and eat.

PAUL: Thanks.

JANE: Paul, what do you think—I'm gonna jure.

PAUL: You're what? Make that a large orange juice, willya, Jane? Gotta big day ahead of me.

ACE: Big day—what's going on today—blasting?

PAUL: Oh we're through blasting.

ACE: I'm glad.

PAUL: But the excavating's been held up by the mud—we couldn't get the trucks in and out.

ACE: We couldn't.

PAUL: Had a lot of excitement around there the past week—
there was a truck pulling out—

JANE: Paul, don't you wanta hear about my juring?

PAUL: Oh yeh, sis—what's up?

JANE: I'm gonna be on a jury. Somebody's suing somebody
for some money in the gum machine, and I have to decide
how much money he gets or not. But I have to be on a
bias.

ACE: Isn't that awful?

JANE: Oh I don't think so, dear. Three dollars a day is not
to be sneezed.

PAUL: Three bucks a day—can this big, rich city afford that?
Pass the eggs, Jane.

JANE: Help yourself, Paul.

PAUL: Three measly dollars a day—so you're on a jury two
weeks, you wind up with a measly thirty dollars, that kills
me.

ACE: Paul have you got change for a quarter?

PAUL: Change? No, I don't think I—

ACE: Never mind. I gotta get going, Jane. I'll call you.

JANE: Yes, you call me. I'll let you know how I'm doing. Call
me at the courthouse about noon.

ACE: Oh sure—the judge'll run down to the candy store and
take a message.

MUSIC BRIDGE

ACE: Well Jane weighed in on the scales of justice at 105,

wearing purple trunks and an off-the-face hat. In the other corner, in the black robe, her very capable opponent, the judge, at 178—that's blood pressure. The first day's court procedure went something like this:

ECHO CHAMBER . . . GAVEL

JUDGE: The bailiff will call the next name . . . let's impanel this jury and get on with the case. How many more do we need, clerk?

CLERK: One more, your honor.

JUDGE: Call the next name.

CLERK: Mr. Witley, step into the jury box, please.

WITLEY: (OFF) Yes sir— (FOOTSTEPS)

JUDGE: Mr. Brown as counsel for the plaintiff, question this last one briefly, please?

BROWN: I'll try your honor. Mr. Witley—is that your name?

WITLEY: That's me.

BROWN: You are acquainted with the nature of this case by now, I presume.

WITLEY: Yes sir. Autombile accident.

BROWN: That's right—my client is suing the trucking company for damages resulting from a truck backing into his automobile. Now, Mr. Witley, is there any reason you can not give a fair decision in this trial?

WITLEY: I should say I can give a fair decision. I've been waiting for a chance like this. Two years ago one of them trucks backed into me—and I didn't collect a cent. Now I've got a chance to—

BROWN: You're excused.

WITLEY: What?

BROWN: I say you're excused—you won't do. (GAVEL)

JUDGE: Step down, Mr. Witley. Clerk, call the next name.

CLERK: Mrs. Jane Ace, please. (FOOTSTEPS)

JANE: Well, finally. It's about time you got to me. I get up at the crank of dawn and I have to sit around— (GAVEL)

JUDGE: Stop that muttering. Step into the jury box.

CLERK: Seat twelve, Mrs. Ace.

JANE: Oh, right on the aisle.

BROWN: Mrs. Ace—is that your name?

JANE: I do.

BROWN: What?

JANE: I said I do. (GAVEL)

JUDGE: You do what? Put your hand down.

JANE: Well don't you have to hold up your right hand and— (GAVEL)

JUDGE: I said put your hand down. And sit down.

JANE: Yes sir.

BROWN: Mrs. Ace, I'm Mr. Brown, counsel for the plaintiff. Is there any reason you cannot give a fair decision in this trial?

JANE: Oh no, Mr. Brown.

BROWN: Good. Now—

JANE: What's the trial about?

BROWN: What?

JANE: I was sitting so far back there I couldn't see exactly what was—

BROWN: This is an action involving damages in a collision between a truck backing out of a passageway and crashing into the plaintiff's car.

JANE: My goodness—was he hurt?

BROWN: Was he hur—well he's suing for ten thousand dollars damages.

JANE: Ten thousand dol—what kind of a car was it, Mr. Brown?

BROWN: It wasn't the car so much—the plaintiff was seriously — (GAVEL)

JUDGE: We'll discuss the details in the course of the trial. Get to the point.

BROWN: Mrs. Ace, have you ever been in an automobile accident?

JANE: Oh no—knock wood. (KNOCKS WOOD)

BROWN: That's good enough for me. If the court please, the jury is satisfactory to me.

JUDGE: Good. It's about time. Is the jury satisfactory to counsel for defendant?

BAKER: Yes, it is, your honor.

JUDGE: You are Miss Baker, aren't you?

BAKER: Yes your honor. I represent the defendant. The jury is satisfactory to me.

JUDGE: Very well. (SOUND OF FINGER SNAPPING) We will proceed with the case. Counsel for the—counsel for the—will juror number twelve kindly lower her hand and stop snapping her fingers at the court.

JANE: But judge, I wanted to ask you something. I'm expecting a phone call from my husband. So if he calls—

JUDGE: Phone call!

JANE: Yes, he said he'd call me here to find out how I made out. So if it comes, will you call me? I'll be sitting right here in seat twelve.

JUDGE: Mrs.—uh—what is that name?

JANE: Mrs. Ace. My husband is Mr. Ace.

JUDGE: Mrs. Ace, the court will not permit you to receive personal communications interfering with the orderly conduct of this trial. The court will not tolerate any such action.

JANE: Well you're the judge here, couldn't you ask the court to call me to the—

JUDGE: I *am* the court!

JANE: *You're* the court!

JUDGE: I am. (GAVEL) Sit down.

JANE: I thought this room was the court. In *The Paradine Case*, which I saw three times—

JUDGE: Did you hear me tell you to sit down?

JANE: But if a person can't get a phone call—

JUDGE: Mrs. Ace, do you realize there is a ten-thousand-dollar law action about to take place here?

JANE: Yes, but I told my husband to call me up when—

BAKER: If it please the court—

JUDGE: What is it, Miss Baker?

BAKER: Your honor if this juror is going to sit through this trial, her mind occupied with the ringing of a phone bell—

JUDGE: There will be no phone bells in this courtroom.

JANE: But judge— (GAVEL)

JUDGE: Sit down. (WILL I CALL HER TO THE PHONE) This is a court of law. I've been on the bench for thirty-five years, and I've never heard of such a request. It's either insolence or downright ignorance. And before you're finished in this courtroom, Mrs. Ace, you will at least have absorbed some of the decorum congruous to judicial dignity.

JANE: How was that again?

BROWN: Your honor, as counsel for the plaintiff, I would like to open my case.

JUDGE: Oh, you would!

BAKER: Your honor, I ask for a recess. The defendant is trying to locate a surprise witness.

JUDGE: Telephone calls—surprise witnesses—you people see too many movies. The court is in no mood to hear this case now. But before adjourning for the day, I wish to instruct the jury not to discuss this case among themselves or by telephone. I mean among themselves or with anyone else. The jury will phone me tomorrow—that is, the jury will report tomorrow morning at ten o'clock, and I expect every juror to be in the phone booth ready to—I mean in the jury bo—oh, what's the use. (GAVEL) Court is adjourned.

MUSIC BRIDGE

ACE: Well, that was Jane's first day in court . . . Oh well, another day, another three dollars. (CASH REGISTER) Thank you, Mr. Mayor . . . That night after dinner at home, I tried to get Jane to give me all the dope on the case. But the dope on the case had another problem she was wrestling with:

JANE: Three dollars a day—times two hundred and eighty days to Christmas. That would be—

ACE: Jane, you don't think the trial is going to last to Christmas, do you?

JANE: It might—the way that judge picks on everything that comes up.

ACE: For instance.

JANE: Yes . . . Three times 280 is—

ACE: That's going to come to a lot of money, Jane.

JANE: It's nothing compared to what she's going to get. She's suing for ten thousand dollars in an automobile accident.

ACE: Who's she?

JANE: Miss Baker, I think her name is. She doesn't seem to have been hurt very much—she's very attractive—tall, dark, no nail polish . . . But I'm disappointed, dear.

ACE: In what?

JANE: I thought it would be a more exciting case. A murder or at least something interesting. Who cares about a truck? They said something about a surprise witness to-morrow—I hope that makes it more exciting.

ACE: Oh a truck driver is the defendant? And Miss Baker, is the plaintiff?

JANE: Uh—yes, one of those. It's kinda mixed up. And that judge—he's all over the place. If it isn't one thing, it's me.

ACE: *You?*

JANE: Oh, all right, it's I. Fine time to pick on my grammar. Let me see, three dollars a day times two hundred and eighty days to Christmas—

ACE: Jane, I still don't quite get the case. This Miss Baker was driving her car and a truck ran into her? Who's her lawyer?

JANE: Mr. Brown, I think.

ACE: You think?

JANE: Dear, I told you it's all kinda mixed up. And I've gotta figure out how much profit I'm gonna make. And besides the judge told us not to talk about the case to anybody or on the phone.

ACE: What's that?

JANE: Look, dear, if you wanta know more about it, come down to the court and watch me jure.

ACE: I might just do that.

JANE: They have a studio audience. But don't ask the judge for any phone calls.

ACE: Phone calls?

JANE: I did. He blew up higher than a hall.

ACE: Jane, you mean you asked the—

JANE: Dear, please—while I'm on this jury, I can't talk. Just be good enough to say "Hello, Jane," and that's all.

ACE: Just, Hello Jane.

JANE: Just those three words—Hell-o, Jane.

MUSIC BRIDGE

ACE: The next morning before I left the house, Jane made me promise to come down to watch, and I left her with three words—Bon jure, Jane. She picked up a free ride downtown that morning from our next-door neighbor, Ken Roberts. He's the radio announcer. As Ken was getting into his car he saw Jane leaving the house for court—I *thought* it was for court, I didn't know a new complication had set in.

KEN: Hey, Jane, what have you been doing?

JANE: Just fine, Ken?

KEN: Well, how are you?

JANE: I've been serving on a jury. I'm going downtown now.

KEN: Well, I'm driving downtown, Jane.

JANE: Oh, I'll be glad to. Thanks, Ken. (AUTO DOOR OPENS)

KEN: Hop right in. Which courthouse you going to? (DOOR CLOSES AND MOTOR STARTS)

JANE: Well, I'm not going right to the courthouse. I have an appointment at the hair dresser this morning, and I asked Sally to take my place on the jury in case I'm a little late. My cousin, Sally Anderson.

KEN: Oh yes, Mr. Ace's secretary.

JANE: I may be five or ten minutes late, and I don't want them to wait for me. I told Sally to be there at ten sharp. I just *have* to get to a beauty shop. My goodness, yesterday I looked like the wrath of grapes, next to that Miss Baker.

KEN: There's nothing wrong with the way you look today, Jane.

JANE: You do? Well thanks, Ken, but I had this appointment —I don't suppose they mind if Sally fills in for me for a few minutes. If the judge wants me to, I'll stay overtime to make up for it.

ACE: If I were a nice guy I'd spare you this next courtroom scene entirely. But I'm slightly sadistic . . . translation, I'm a heel . . . I *will* warn you, though, to move back a little from your radios—because when Judge Edwards gets a load of Jane's substitute in the jury box, I wouldn't want any of it to get on you.

ECHO CHAMBER

JUDGE: We will proceed with the case on trial. Counsel for the plaintiff will open the case. Are you ready?

JENKINS: Thank you, Judge Edwards. I am.

JUDGE: Just a minute—who are you—I thought Mr. Brown was counsel for plaintiff.

JENKINS: I'm Mr. Jenkins, Mr. Brown's partner. We're both handling this case.

JUDGE: Very well, proceed.

JENKINS: Thank you, Judge Edwards. And if it please the
court, ladies and gentlemen of the jury. The plaintiff
in this case, Thomas Mason, is suing the defendant for
injuries received from a truck loaded with brick and dirt,
backing out of a building project without an attendant
to flag passing motorists. Mr. Mason received such injuries as to necessitate two months' confinement in the
hospital, and a month's convalescence in his home, to
say nothing of such shock and nervous disorder as to
incapacitate his regular attendance to the work by which
until three months ago he earned his livelihood. (DOOR
OPENS AND CLOSES AND FOOTSTEPS APPROACH UNDER DIA-
LOGUE) You will learn in the course of this trial that the
injuries received by the plaintiff were so serious as to
cause his physician to despair of his complete recovery.

JANE: OK, Sally, I'm here.

ANDERSON: Oh, hello, Jane.

JANE: Am I very late?

ANDERSON: No, that man just started to— (GAVEL)

JUDGE: What's going on back there?

JANE: It's all right, Judge—it's only me. I'm back.

JUDGE: Back!

JANE: Yes, I let my cousin Sally jure in my place while I
went to the beauty shop. OK, Sally, I'll sit in there now.
You can sit out there and watch if you like.

ANDERSON: It's a kinda dull case, Jane. (GAVEL)

JUDGE: Mrs. Ace, what is the meaning of this?

JANE: Well, like I told you, Mr. Edwards—

JUDGE: *Mr.* Edwards! I am Judge William Edwards. You will never refer to me as Mr. Edwards.

JANE: Well thank you, William, and you may call me— (LAUGHS . . . GAVEL)

JUDGE: Silence—order—quiet—stop that laughing. I will not tolerate these outbursts in my court. I will clear this courtroom if this continues. Now, Mrs. Ace—

JANE: Yes.

JUDGE: Yes, Your Honor.

JANE: Yes, my Honor. (LAUGHS AND GAVEL AGAIN)

JUDGE: Order—order in this court. Did you hear me say I'll clear the courtroom if there is another outburst? We are here on serious business—and it will be the duty of this court to see that you observe proper court etiquette —and putting an added starter in the jury box is not proper court etiquette.

BAKER: Your Honor, I move for a mistrial. (GAVEL)

JUDGE: Oh, you do, Miss Baker. Well, I say there will be no mistrial.

BAKER: But Your Honor, if a juror is not—

JUDGE: Sit down. And you too, Mrs. Ace—sit down.

ANDERSON: So long, Jane. Your hair looks wonderful. Too good for *this* trial.

JANE: You do? I was in such a hurry— (GAVEL)

JUDGE: Silence. Stop that chattering. And let's get on with this case. Mr. Jenkins, Counsel for the Plaintiff will proceed.

JENKINS: Yes, Your Honor. As I was saying, ladies and gentlemen of the jury—

JANE: Mr. Jenkins! I thought Mr. *Brown* was the lawyer.
(GAVEL)

JUDGE: What was that—what did she say?

JANE: I said I thought Mr. Brown was the lawyer. Who's
Mr. Jenkins? Is he the surprise witness we've been waiting for?

JUDGE: Mrs. Ace, if you had been here when court opened
you would have been apprised of the fact, that Mr.
Jenkins and Mr. Brown are handling this case.

JENKINS: Yes, Mrs. Ace, you see Mr. Brown and I are partners-
in-law.

JANE: Partners-in-law? Oh, that's cute—you both married sis-
ters! (LAUGHTER) (GAVEL AGAIN)

JUDGE: Order—order in this courtroom. That does it—I warned
you—*Clerk!*

CLERK: Yes, Your Honor.

JUDGE: Clear this court of all spectators. Everybody out. Get
everybody out of this courtroom.

CLERK: All right—everybody out— (SOUND OF FEET AND VOICES)
—clear the court—step lively—that's it— (SOUNDS FADE OUT
AND DOOR CLOSES) —OK, Your Honor, they're all out.

JUDGE: Now we'll see if we can get some decorum here. Mr.
Jenkins proceed.

JENKINS: Yes, Your Honor. Ladies and gentlemen of the jury,
as I pointed out, the defendant received such injuries and
such shock as to—as to—as to—

JUDGE: Well, well—go on—what's the matter with you?

JENKINS: But your honor there are only eleven jurors in that box.

JUDGE: What? Eleven jur—where is she—clerk! (GAVEL)

CLERK: Yes, Your Honor.

JUDGE: Find that woman.

CLERK: She must have thought you meant her when you said everybody out. (GAVEL)

JUDGE: *Find* her—bring her back here—and keep hunting till you do find her.

MUSIC BRIDGE

ACE: This, I am happy to say, I was spared. I had decided to come watch Jane later that afternoon. The next scene of this harrowing story takes place a few minutes later in a courtroom upstairs from Judge Edwards. *Another* trial by jury is taking place:

ECHO CHAMBER . . . GAVEL TWICE

MORLEY: Counsel will proceed with the witness.

LAWYER: Thank you, Judge Morley. Now Miss Delmar, I want to ask you to look at this letter—do you recognize the handwriting?

DELMAR: I do.

LAWYER: Whose handwriting is it?

DELMAR: (SOFTLY) Mine.

LAWYER: Louder please, so the jury can hear you, Miss Delmar.

MORLEY: Yes, the witness will be a little more distinct. Counsel will put the question again.

LAWYER: Whose handwriting is it, Miss Delmar?

DELMAR: (LOUD) I said it was mine. Did you hear that?

LAWYER: Thank you, Miss Delmar. I shall now read it. "*My darling perfect man. I'll be there again tonight. Waiting. Waiting. Will you ever come to me? Signed Irene.* And then there follows a most peculiar series of X's. I wonder what they could mean. I wish to pass this letter among you ladies and gentlemen of the jury. Mr. Foreman, would you read this and pass it along? And as you read it, ladies and gentlemen, kindly keep in mind that this letter was written by a woman who says she loved her husband.

DELMAR: I do. I do love my husband.

LAWYER: Of course you do. I just told the jury you do. Of course, it is a little strange that you should be writing that letter to another man—who was murdered—the letter which the jury is now reading—oh have you all read this?

JANE: I haven't read it.

LAWYER: Oh I beg your pardon, madame. Will you please pass this back to juror number—juror number— (GAVEL)

MORLEY: Well what is it—what's holding things up down there?

LAWYER: Your honor, there are thirteen jurors in the box. (SOUND OF VOICES)

MORLEY: What's that? Thirteen jurors.

LAWYER: The lady sitting on the rail back there.

MORLEY: What? Madame—how'd *you* get in here? Are you a juror?

JANE: Yes, I am.

MORLEY: What seat do you occupy in the box?

JANE: Oh, no seat—it was crowded so I sat up on this railing back here—

LAWYER: I move for a mistrial. (MUMBLE OF VOICES . . . GAVEL)

MORLEY: Motion denied. And I want this courtroom quiet, or I'll clear everybody out of the room.

JANE: Oh now don't *you* start that *too*. Judge Edwards just chased me out of his jury.

MORLEY: What's that?

JANE: I was juring downstairs and Judge Edwards chased us all out. So I came up here—this is a much more interesting trial.

MORLEY: Madame, get out of that jury box. (FOOTSTEPS) And get right down to Judge Edwards' court.

JANE: I don't like that case down there. It's just an old automobile accident. Would somebody in this jury like to swap cases? (LAUGHS . . . GAVEL)

JUDGE: *Order!* Quiet! And as for you, madame, another word out of you, and you'll be held in contempt of *two* courts at the same *time* . . . Two courts—I never even heard of *that*—more new things happening these days. Get down stairs to that other court. You hear me.

ACE: While Jane was wandering around the halls of justice

shopping for a spicy lamour to jure, her stand-in, Miss Anderson, had come back to my office and explained why she was late. By the time she got to the part where Jane had called the judge William, I was in a cab on my way to the courthouse with ten thousand dollars bail money, which I happened to have in my pocket at the time.

ECHO CHAMBER . . . FOOTSTEPS

JANE: (FADES HERSELF ON) Well, Judge Edwards, I'm back again, and I can't say I'm too happy to be back here. There's a much more interesting case going on upstairs.

JUDGE: Mrs. Ace!

JANE: Yes?

JUDGE: How dare you walk out of that jury box?

JANE: Well, when you said everybody out, I was under the impersonation you meant me, too. So I went upstairs. What a letter they read up there! You don't have any letters down here—what you need down here is love interest—

BAKER: Your honor, may I interrupt? (GAVEL)

JUDGE: You may not, Miss Baker.

BAKER: But I only wanted to say that the defendant's surprise witness has arrived and we're ready to proceed with the case.

JANE: Surprise witness? Well, maybe this case'll get more interesting.

JUDGE: Mrs. Ace, you try my patience.

JANE: All right. (GAVEL)

JUDGE: Get back there in that jury box.

JANE: Yes sir. (FOOTSTEPS)

JUDGE: And I warn you one more word out of you, and I'll throw the book at you.

JANE: (OFF) You might hit an innocent by-sitter, judge.

JUDGE: *Sit down!* I warned you now. Just sit down there.

JANE: I'm sitting.

JUDGE: Now bring on this so called surprise witness—more movie stuff—call the witness.

BAKER: I call Paul Sherwood to the stand.

CLERK: Paul Sherwood take the stand. (FOOTSTEPS)

PAUL: (OFF) Coming.

JANE: Paul Sherwood! (GAVEL)

JUDGE: Mrs. Ace—I warned you!

JANE: But Judge, Paul Sherwood is my— (GAVEL)

JUDGE: *Quiet!* Miss Baker, you may question your witness.

BAKER: Mr. Sherwood, where were you on the morning of December 16th?

PAUL: Well, I was down at the place—that excavation on 45th Street—and when this truck backed out, the man who usually flags it wasn't there. I remember that distinctly.

BAKER: How do you remember that so distinctly?

PAUL: Well this particular morning I was late getting down there, and somebody else was standing at my peephole, because I had breakfast at my sister's and the toaster wasn't working, and I had to—

JANE: Oh I remember that morning— (GAVEL)

JUDGE: Mrs. Ace, that does it.

JANE: But judge, the witness is my brother. I remember—

JUDGE: I don't care if he's your brother . . . Brother?

JANE: If I'd have known *that* was gonna be the surprise, I'd have—

JENKINS: Your honor, I move for a mistrial.

JUDGE: Oh yes? Well before we do that, I'm gonna make an example of that woman.

ACE: (OFF) Your Honor, may I say a word here?

JANE: Dear! You here, too?

JUDGE: What? Who's *this* man? How'd he get here?

ACE: I'm her husband, Your Honor.

JUDGE: Oh so you're her husband. You're fined fifty dollars.

ACE: For what?

JUDGE: For being her husband. (GAVEL) And I hereby declare this case a mistrial. It's all because of this woman, Mrs. Ace, who should never be allowed in a jury box again, and if I had my way she would never even be allowed to vote because this will go down in the records of jurisprudence as the most ridiculous mistrial of 1948. Do you understand that, Mrs. Ace?

JANE: Yes sir, I've just been voted Miss Trial of 1948. (GAVEL)

JUDGE: Court's adjourned.

JANE THINKS MINK

JANE: You like this picture of me?

ACE: Excellent.

JANE: You do? I do, too. I had to look high and dry, but I finally found it. There's a lot of them there. Shall I get them?

ACE: Jane, we better concentrate on the scripts. We've got *thousands* of scripts.

JANE: Well, you know what they say—a thousand pictures are better than one word. I'll go get another favorite of mine.

ACE: OK, and while you're looking, I'll forge ahead here.

MUSIC: MANHATTAN SERENADE.
ACE: *Ladies and gentlemen, Easy Aces.*
MUSIC OUT

ACE: I ran across an interesting quotation the other day—I'd like to read it to you. *No man is an island entire of itself. Every man is a piece of the continent, a part of the main* . . . Fine way to start a comedy program—

what's happening to radio? . . Well to tell the truth I didn't know exactly what it meant myself, so I read it aloud to Jane, and she said:

JANE: Do you think I oughta let out the hem on this dress some more?

ACE: And she's so right . . . Now there is a woman who lives on an island all by herself. Up around Lake Marijuana. But, back to the quotation. No man is an island—particularly on Manhattan. Because our lives are knitted together in one stitched pattern. What you do depends on what I do—what I do depends on what Jane does—oops, dropped a stitch . . . What happened to me this past week demonstrates what I mean. You see when Jane and I think of buying something expensive, we talk it over. For instance, when we thought of buying a used car, we found it wasn't what it was cracked up to be.

JANE: We thought of buying a used car, but it wasn't what it was jacked up to be.

ACE: Even when Jane goes to buy lingerie, I make very good suggestions.

JANE: Even when I go to buy lingerie, he's very suggestive.

ACE: One of us never does anything without letting the other one know.

JANE: One of us never does anything without letting me know.

ACE: The other night after dinner I was sitting around reading the paper, and Jane was going over her shopping list for the next day:

JANE: Now let me see if I've got everything down that I want to buy tomorrow: toothbrush, soap, cleansing cream, mink coat, and lipstick . . . Anything you need dear?

ACE: Uh—yes it has been.

JANE: Dear, you're not listening—put the paper away. Look at my shopping list—see if you wanta add anything.

ACE: Let me see—toothbrush, soap, cleansing cream, mink coat, and lipstick. No I don't need anything. Unless you wanta return those ginger ale bottles—we get a nickel back on each bottle and every little bit will— *Help! Mink coat!* What is this thing here?

JANE: Where? Oh yes, mink coat—I meant to talk to you about that. Make a lap, dear.

ACE: What?

JANE: Make a lap, I wanta sit down.

ACE: OK, I made a lap, but you're not gonna—

JANE: There now, isn't this cozy? Oh look dear, your lap's getting a front porch here.

ACE: Yes, and if you'll look around in back you'll find a veranda. Now Jane, about this coat—

JANE: Dear, I saw it again today. It's a dream. You know that fur shop around the corner?

ACE: Just to say hello to.

JANE: Well, I've been passing it every day, and there's this dreamy mink coat in the window. The girl wearing it looks so smart. Of course she's just a dummy. And so could I.

ACE: How much?

JANE: It's full length and it'll cover all my dresses.

ACE: How much?

JANE: It's the softest mink. It's wild.

ACE: Who isn't! How much, Jane?

JANE: That's just it. You haven't heard the half of it.

ACE: Well, how much?

JANE: Seventeen hundred and fifty dollars.

ACE: That's pretty reasonable for a good mink coat.

JANE: Now you've heard the half of it. All together it's thirty-five hundred.

ACE: What?

JANE: Now dear, take it easy—relapse. Remember your blood pleasure.

ACE: Look, Jane, let's be reasonable. Where am I gonna get that kind of money?

JANE: I knew you were gonna say that. I knew it.

ACE: But Jane, you know we can't afford to spend all that money—

JANE: Everybody gets some pleasure out of our money but me. How about your sister's oldest boy when he had his tonsils out—and your brother's youngest girl when she had her adenoids out. *You* paid for all that. Everybody has a wonderful time on our money but me.

ACE: What wonderful times? Only—

JANE: And how about your mother's teeth? Who paid for that?

ACE: Leave my mother's teeth out of this.

JANE: Oh when I mention your mother's teeth they hurt . . . I suppose *you'll* be happy if I don't have a fur coat, and get pneumonia and have to spend the winter in an oxydol tent.

ACE: That's a sparkling notion. Jane, look, tell you what I'm gonna do.

JANE: Oh, I knew you would, dear.

ACE: Wait a minute now—listen to this. I've got a big advertising account coming up. Pretty good chance of getting it. It's for the Royal Paint Company. If I get it, there'll be a bonus in it for me and then you can have the mink coat.

JANE: Oh thanks, dear.

ACE: *Wait*—I said *if* I get the account. I have a fifty percent chance of getting it.

JANE: That's only the half of it, dear. You'll get it. You'll get it by hook or ladder. And if I'm wrong I'm not far from it.

MUSIC BRIDGE

ACE: When I told Jane there was a fifty percent chance of getting the account, I wasn't kidding. The other fifty percent depended on how good business got at the Royal Paint Company—in fact there was a certain color the paint company hoped to be out of the . . . red, if I'm not too subversive . . . But no paint company is an island entire of itself. Watch how this pattern begins to weave. After I left for the office the next morning, Jane got busy on the telephone:

JANE: Hello, is this the Daniels Fur Shop?

DANIELS: (FILTER) Yes, Mr. Daniels speaking.

JANE: Oh, I didn't recognize your voice. This is Mrs. Ace.

DANIELS: Oh, Mrs. Ace, I didn't recognize you, either.

JANE: Just fine . . . Mr. Daniels, remember that mink coat I've been looking at?

DANIELS: I certainly do. A lot of women have been looking at it.

JANE: Yes it certainly is . . . Well, Mr. Daniels, could you hold that coat for me?

DANIELS: You mean you're buying it?

JANE: Well, practically.

DANIELS: What do you mean practically?

JANE: Well I talked to my husband about it last night. And he said it's sixty percent certain I can buy it.

DANIELS: Well, good for you, Mrs. Ace. That is, if he'll really let you buy it.

JANE: Oh, I'm sure he will. Because if he didn't want me he would have come right out flatheaded and said so . . . Doesn't it to you?

DANIELS: Tell you what, I don't usually hold coats without at least a deposit, but I have a certain reason for doing it for you. Because if you buy this coat it'll come in mighty handy. My wife'll be thrilled to hear about this. I'm gonna call her now and tell her. (DIALS)

MUSIC BRIDGE

MARY: (FILTER) Hello.

DANIELS: Hello, Mrs. Daniels?

MARY: Yes this is Mrs. Daniels.

DANIELS: Mrs. Daniels, this is a man named Daniels who claims to be married to you.

MARY: Oh hello, John, you silly thing.

DANIELS: Oh silly, am I? Not too silly to buy you that home out in the suburbs you've been wanting so bad.

MARY: John! Not really.

DANIELS: *Now* who's silly.

MARY: Oh John you don't mean it—are we really finally gonna buy it?

DANIELS: Well it's practically ours, honey.

MARY: Oh practically—what do you mean, practically ours?

DANIELS: Well, I'd say it's seventy percent ours.

MARY: Seventy percent?

DANIELS: You know that mink coat I've had in the shop so long—well, Mrs. Ace just called me and said her husband told her he was seventy percent certain she could have it.

MARY: But that's not definite, John.

DANIELS: But Mary, if he didn't want her to have it wouldn't he have come out flatheaded and said she couldn't have it?

MARY: What?

DANIELS: Doesn't it to you?

MARY: John, you're so excited.

DANIELS: I certainly am—we've been dreaming about that house for sometime now. You go right ahead and plan on it.

MARY: Oh, John, you're a darling. In fact Mr. Beckley from the real estate office called me just a little while ago about the house. I told him to give us another day or two to think it over—and he was so understanding. Will he be surprised when I call him back now!

MUSIC BRIDGE

BECKLEY: (FILTER) Beckley real estate, Mr. Beckley speaking.

MARY: Hello, Mr. Beckley, this is Mrs. Daniels again.

BECKLEY: Oh hello, Mrs. Daniels—got some good news for me?

MARY: I think I have. If you call it good news that we're gonna buy that house.

BECKLEY: Well, congratulations, Mrs. Daniels. Your husband changed his mind rather suddenly, didn't he?

MARY: He certainly did. But the house is practically ours now.

BECKLEY: What do you mean, practically?

MARY: Well, Mr. Daniels just phoned me. He said it was eighty percent certain.

BECKLEY: Eighty percent? That's not a hundred, Mrs. Daniels.

MARY: Well, if he didn't want me to buy it wouldn't he have come out flatheaded and said so?

BECKLEY: Haha, you're a little excited, aren't you, Mrs. Daniels?

MARY: Well, doesn't it to you?

BECKLEY: Yes, I must admit it does. Or did—or—what was the question?

MARY: I said it's as certain as anything could be. And Mr. Beckley, I want to remind you that you promised to fix it up in good shape. It certainly needs a lot of renovating. I'll be out this afternoon and sign the papers and give you a deposit.

BECKLEY: Good. And don't worry about renovating—it's going to be painted thoroughly—as a matter of fact that's the last house we have in that subdivision out there and now that you're gonna buy it, I'm going to order a paint job for every house out there. In fact I feel safe enough now in calling the paint people and putting in the order.

MUSIC BRIDGE

GIRL: Royal Paint Company, good morning.

BECKLEY: This is Mr. Beckley—may I speak to Mr. Benson? He knows what it's about.

GIRL: (FILTER) Just a moment please. (CLICK)

BENSON: (FILTER) Benson speaking.

BECKLEY: Oh good morning, Mr. Benson. This is Beckley out on the island.

BENSON: Oh yes, Mr. Beckley—what's the good word this morning?

BECKLEY: The good word is that I'm gonna put through that paint order.

BENSON: Yeh? You finally got rid of that last house out there, huh?

BECKLEY: Well it's about ninety percent certain.

BENSON: Ninety percent?

BECKLEY: Well, I mean the woman's husband didn't come out flatheaded and say no.

BENSON: You're a little worked up, aren't you?

BECKLEY: I certainly am. Now I'm giving you this order in plenty of time—I oughta get delivery on the paint pretty quick, doesn't it to you?

BENSON: It certainly does—I mean, yes it will. Or something. And that reminds me—I'm glad you called. I've been waiting to hear from you on this order before I did something myself. I gotta make a call. Thanks for the order, Beckley.

MUSIC BRIDGE

ACE: (FILTER) Yes, this is Mr. Ace.

BENSON: This is Benson, Royal Paint.

ACE: Oh yes, Mr. Benson—what's new?

BENSON: Well, looks like we're gonna do some advertising.

ACE: Really? Gee, that's swell—I was just sitting here working out an idea for you.

BENSON: Good. It's ninety-nine percent certain. I can tell you now the reason I've been hesitating. We've been waiting on a pretty big paint order, and it looks now like we're gonna get it. As I say it's ninety-nine percent certain. I'll call you about three or four o'clock this afternoon and give you the definite OK.

ACE: Well, I think we can push that other one per cent over by three or four o'clock.

BENSON: That's the way I feel. If the man I was waiting for to come across with the order wasn't going to buy the paint, he'd have come out flatheaded and said so. Doesn't it to you?

ACE: Oh sure, Ja— Mr. Benson—what did you say?

BENSON: Tell you what we wanna do, Mr. Ace. I'd like to have you concentrate on one particular quality of our paint—it's a one coat paint.

ACE: One coat? That's funny.

BENSON: What?

ACE: Nothing—I was just thinking of that one coat—that kinda reminds me of something I was talking to Mrs. Ace about last night. I'll be working on an idea, Mr. Benson. I've gotta make a call right now.

MUSIC BRIDGE

JANE: (FILTER) Hello.

ACE: Hello Jane, guess what.

JANE: You mean guess who, don't you dear?

ACE: No, I mean guess what happened—got a call from the paint company—and the deal is ninety-nine and three quarters percent certain.

JANE: Oh that's a shame. I wanted a full length coat—not three quarters.

ACE: Isn't that awful. It looks like I'm gonna get their advertising. The guy didn't turn me down, Jane—he didn't come right out flatfooted and say no.

JANE: Oh that's wonderful. You mean I can—

ACE: You certainly can. I promised you. Better wait till about three or four o'clock, huh? I expect to get a call from Mr. Benson definitely OK-ing the deal by that time.

JANE: Three or four o'clock—OK, dear—I'll be waiting on pins and cushions.

MUSIC BRIDGE

ACE: Well, three o'clock came—four o'clock came—my shadow came—and still no call from the Royal Paint Company. How was I to know he was waiting to hear from somebody else who was waiting to hear from somebody else who was waiting to hear from Jane, who was waiting to hear from me? A sort of Tinkers to Evers to fifty percent chance . . . How vicious can a circle be? . . . Finally I decided to take a chance myself. I called the Royal Paint Company.

GIRL: (FILTER) Royal Paint Company.

ACE: This is Mr. Ace. May I speak to Mr. Benson, please?

GIRL: Just a moment, Mr. Ace. (CLICK)

BENSON: (FILTER) Benson speaking.

ACE: This is Mr. Ace—I didn't get your call and I thought I'd take a chance. You said it was ninety-nine percent certain—

BENSON: Well it was. But I've been waiting to hear from a certain party and I haven't heard from him. I think I'll give him a ring right now, Mr. Ace, and find out what's going on.

MUSIC BRIDGE

BENSON: Is that you, Mr. Beckley?

BECKLEY: (FILTER) Yes, who is this?

BENSON: This is Mr. Benson—what happened on that paint order?

BECKLEY: Well, I've been waiting to hear from that woman who was gonna buy that house. She told me it was ninety percent certain. I think I'll give her a ring and see what's going on.

MUSIC BRIDGE

MARY: (FILTER) Yes, this is Mrs. Daniels.

BECKLEY: Oh, Mrs. Daniels, this Mr. Beckley—How about that house—weren't you coming over to sign the papers and make a deposit?

MARY: Well I was, Mr. Beckley, I was eighty percent certain I was. But I've been waiting to hear from my husband.

I haven't heard from him all day. I'll tell you what I'll do Mr. Beckley—I'll give him a ring and I'll be back to you very soon.

MUSIC BRIDGE

DANIELS: (FILTER) But honey, I expected to hear from Mrs. Ace and she hasn't called me. She told me it was seventy percent certain.

MARY: Well Mr. Beckley is calling me like mad, John—

DANIELS: I'll call up Mrs. Ace and find out what goes on. See you later, honey.

MUSIC BRIDGE

JANE: (FILTER) But, Mr. Daniels, I've been waiting on pins and cushions all afternoon to hear from my husband. He said it was sixty percent certain.

DANIELS: Well, why hasn't he called?

JANE: But he hasn't called me up. I've been sitting at this phone till I'm black and blue. I even took four showers.

DANIELS: Four showers!

JANE: The phone always rings when I'm in the shower.

DANIELS: And he hasn't called you?

JANE: No, he hasn't.

DANIELS: Mrs. Ace, you're not kidding me, are you? Are you sure your husband didn't say no? Come clean now.

JANE: Come clean! Mr. Daniels, I *told* you about the four

showers . . . I'm going to call up Mr. Ace and see what's
going on or not.

MUSIC BRIDGE

ACE: (FILTER) No, Jane, I haven't heard from him. If I had,
I'd have called you. I phoned him and told him to let
me know and he hasn't called me. Looks like the coat's
off.

JANE: But dear, what'll I tell Mr. Daniels to do with the coat?

ACE: Uh—no comment.

MUSIC BRIDGE

ACE: Are you lost? Well, don't get discouraged. It gets even
more complicated now. Another character has crept into
the melee. That's our next door neighbor, Ken Roberts
. . . The radio announcer . . . remember? Jane is his big-
gest fan. They exchange confidences. This was their latest
exchange.

JANE: So you see, Ken, I'm really in a quarry.

KEN: Well, Jane, I don't like to interfere in anything as
personal as trying to make your husband buy you a mink
coat.

JANE: Yes, Ken, but—go ahead—but what.

KEN: What do you mean but what?

JANE: I don't know, but there's usually a "but" on the end of
"I don't like to interfere." Say it, Ken, but what.

KEN: Nothing. I just don't like to interfere.

JANE: Oh, I thought there was going to be a but.

KEN: No.

JANE: Oh.

KEN: But that reminds me, Jane—

JANE: Yes, yes, I thought so—you don't like to interfere but what.

KEN: But I think if your husband didn't say no exactly, you should have the mink coat. What you ought to do is order it, and then it'll be too late.

JANE: (WAY UP HIGH) *You mean I*—Excuse me, too high—you mean I oughta get the coat without waiting for him to say if I should.

KEN: Well he didn't say no, Jane.

JANE: Well no, but he didn't say yes.

KEN: But he said it was sixty percent certain, you told me.

JANE: Yes, but that leaves about uh—let me see—sixty from one hundred—aught from aught is—

KEN: It's good enough for a good-sized maybe, Jane. And if you ordered the coat, and had your initials put in the satin lining, it would be too late for him to change his mind.

JANE: Oh I couldn't do that, Ken.

KEN: I would if I were you.

JANE: Well if you're gonna talk me into it, Ken, I will.

KEN: Now wait a minute, don't blame me for this. All I said was, if you had your initials put in the lining—

JANE: Get thee behind me satin—Ken, I'm gonna do it. You're a godspend.

MUSIC BRIDGE

ACE: Well if you own any stock in American Tel and Tel, hang on to it. Because here we go again. Jane has made up her mind to buy the coat and is now about to start that business cycle—a cycle built for six.

JANE: Hello, is that you, Mr. Daniels?

DANIELS: (FILTER) That's right.

JANE: Well Mrs. Ace, this is Mr. Daniels.

DANIELS: What did you say?

JANE: Daniels—D-A-N—I mean A-C-E, Daniels. Jane Daniel Jane Ace. Now I've got it.

DANIELS: Oh, yes, Mrs. Ace, am I glad to hear from you.

JANE: Just fine. It's about those initials, Mrs. Daniels. I'll take the coat.

DANIELS: Initials?

JANE: J.A., in the lining—will you put the initials in?

DANIELS: Then your husband said it was all right?

JANE: We'll cross him when we come to it. I'll be down for a fitting and we'll talk it all over.

DANIELS: Gee, that's swell, Mrs. Ace. I'm sure glad you called. I appreciate it. My wife appreciates it. I'll phone her right now.

MUSIC BRIDGE

MARY: (FILTER) John, dear, is it really true?

DANIELS: It sure is honey.

MARY: I'll call Mr. Beckley right away.

BECKLEY: (FILTER) Well Mrs. Daniels, I'm very happy for you.

MARY: Isn't it wonderful, Mr. Beckley?

BECKLEY: And don't you worry about that paint job—I'll attend to it right away.

MUSIC BRIDGE

BENSON: (FILTER) Yes, sir, Mr. Beckley—this is Mr. Benson.

BECKLEY: That order for that paint—it's official now.

BENSON: Well thank you—good. I'll take care of it right away.

MUSIC BRIDGE

ACE: (FILTER) Yes, Mr. Benson, this is Mr. Ace. I was wondering—

BENSON: Sorry to have held you up this way, but I just this minute got the confirmation on that advertising.

ACE: Oh wonderful, Mr. Benson. When can I see you?

BENSON: Well, suppose I drop down to your office first thing in the morning.

ACE: Fine. I'll have some layouts for you—I've got several good ideas for some billboard advertising.

BENSON: Don't forget that one coat of paint.

ACE: Oh yes—that one coat—I mustn't forget that one coat, especially.

MUSIC BRIDGE

ACE: No, no, wait a minute—it's not over. I know the story sounds as if it's finished and Jane gets the coat and I get the account, and at this point I should be saying well we're a little early folks, so hello . . . But you don't know Jane. And I wanta warn you at this point that everything gets a little tricky here. So watch it. Watch it closely, because we won't repeat this. Here we go—I'm sitting in my office after getting the good news about the advertising order for the paint company—when who should come in but—

JANE: Hello, dear.

ACE: Well, Jane. I was just gonna call you.

JANE: Just fine.

ACE: Sit down—whatsa matter? You look a little beat.

JANE: You mean this hangnail expression?

ACE: Yes, that hang—

JANE: Dear, I've done the most terrible thing I ever did in all the years we've been married, and seven months.

ACE: What did you—

JANE: But first I want you to know how terrible I feel about it and I'm gonna cancel it.

ACE: What did you—

JANE: And I also want you to know I didn't do it of my own violation. I was talked into it by somebody I should have known better.

ACE: What did you—

JANE: I realize now I could never wear it with a clear conscience, no matter how cold it gets.

ACE: What did you—oh—you finished? What did you do? Can't wear what? You don't mean you ordered that mink coat without even waiting to find out if my deal went through.

JANE: In other words, yes.

ACE: What other words?

JANE: But don't worry, dear, I'm gonna cancel it. I told him to go ahead with it, but there's still time to stop him. I may have to pay the initial cost.

ACE: The initial cost—

JANE: I told him to put my monocle in the lining.

ACE: Your monocle?

JANE: But I'm gonna cancel the whole thing. And no sooner said the better. Gimme that phone.

ACE: Wait a minute, Jane—wait—put that down. You don't have to cancel it. I just put over that deal I was telling you about. So you can get the coat and wear it with a clear conscience no matter how cold it gets.

JANE: No dear, that's very sweet—but it's too late. I already did the damage, and this is gonna be a lesson to me. A wife must take the bitter with the better I always say. And until things get better, I'll be satisfied with the bitter. Don't you think I better?

ACE: Uh, Jane—look—the deal is made—you can get the coat.

JANE: No dear—not by a bombsight. A person mustn't run around half-crocked buying mink coats.

ACE: Who's half cro—

JANE: I'm gonna teach me a lesson if it's the last thing I do.

ACE: Well, if you insist on canceling the coat, OK—I'm not gonna argue with you. (PHONE UP AND DIALS)

JANE: I'm sorry it has to be this way—P-L-3-6-3-4-and maybe after this I'll remember to at least ask my husband about it—my own flesh and bones—if I keep doing things like this I'll be kissing my happy home—Hello!

DANIELS: (FILTER) This is Mr. Daniels—who is this?

JANE: Oh hello, Mr. Daniels. You know that mink coat I was looking at?

DANIELS: Yes.

JANE: Well I'm not looking at it any more. Cancel it.

DANIELS: Oh this is terrible. Goodbye, Mrs. Ace. I've gotta call my wife.

MUSIC BRIDGE

MARY: (FILTER) Oh no—you can't do that, John.

DANIELS: I'm sorry, Mary, but that woman canceled the mink coat, just now. It's off. Call Beckley and call off the house.

MUSIC BRIDGE

BECKLEY: (FILTER) But, Mrs. Daniels—you can't call it off now. I thought I had the house sold to you.

MARY: And I thought my husband had a mink coat sold, but the customer just canceled it.

BECKLEY: And now you're canceling the house? Oh brother, I've got some canceling to do myself.

MUSIC BRIDGE

BENSON: (FILTER) What's that? What do you mean you don't want the paint?

BECKLEY: I'm sorry but that's the way it is.

BENSON: But you told me you had that house sold out there to a Mrs. Daniels.

BECKLEY: I thought I had it sold to her—just like Mrs. Daniels thought her husband had a mink coat sold to another woman who just called up and canceled the coat.

BENSON: You mean the whole thing depended on somebody's mink coat.

BECKLEY: That's the way it looks. That's why I'm canceling that paint order.

BENSON: Oh that reminds me—I got some canceling to do myself. Goodbye.

MUSIC BRIDGE

ACE: But Mr. Benson, what happened?

JANE: (SOFTLY) What is it, dear?

BENSON: (FILTER) You heard me—the advertising campaign is called off.

ACE: But why—I should get a reason—what am I gonna say around the office here—was it anything I said?

JANE: What is it, dear?

BENSON: No, nothing like that. It's all because—oh you wouldn't believe me, Mr. Ace. It's too fantastic.

JANE: What is it, dear?

ACE: Jane, will you leave me alone—go home.

BENSON: What did you say?

ACE: No, I was just talking to—Mr. Benson, what is this fantastic reason you mentioned?

BENSON: OK, I'll tell you. Mink coat.

ACE: Uh—what?

BENSON: You see, I told you you wouldn't believe it.

ACE: Yes, I will. I just didn't understand you. Sounded as if you said mink coat. Haha—must have it on my mind— what *did* you say?

BENSON: Mink coat.

ACE: Oh. You did say mink coat.

BENSON: I did. Mink coat—mink coat—mink coat! There, I said it again.

ACE: But what about a mink coat? What's that got to do with this advertising campaign for your paint company?

BENSON: OK, you asked for it. Some lunkhead promised his wife a mink coat—then he backed out—so the woman's husband who sells mink coats had *his* wife cancel a house she was going to buy—and the man who was gonna sell the house called *me* up and canceled a big order for paint and now I'm canceling that advertising campaign.

ACE: You mean it all depended on some—

BENSON: Silly, isn't it?

ACE: But Mr. Benson, after all if you want an advertising campaign—

BENSON: Look, old man, there's no use taking it up with me—it all goes back to Mr. Daniels now—if the Daniels fur shop sells that mink coat we can talk business . . . Hello!

ACE: Excuse me, I dropped the phone. Just hold the phone a minute, please.

BENSON: Well, make it snappy.

ACE: Jane.

JANE: Honestly, dear, the way you talk on a phone, nobody can understand what's going on. Can't you use words of more than one cylinder? Dear, what'sa matter? You're as pale as a goat.

ACE: Jane—Jane, did I just hear you call a Mr. Daniels to cancel that mink coat?

JANE: Yes, that's the fur shop around the corner I was telling you about.

ACE: Isn't that awful? Jane, you almost ruined a whole big advertising campaign for me.

JANE: *Me! For you! Me! For you!*

ACE: And me for you, and tea for two.

JANE: How did I do anything to your old advertising campaign? I don't know anything about it.

ACE: I know—and still you almost ruined it.

JANE: How could I do that?

ACE: It's a gift, Jane. . . . (FADING) It's going to be OK on that mink coat paint—I mean that one-coat paint.

MUSIC PLAYOFF

JANE TAKES UP ASTROLOGY

JANE: OK, dear, I found it. It's a picture of Blackie and me.

ACE: Very good.

JANE: Poor little Blackie. I miss him.

ACE: He lived to the ripe old age of thirteen.

JANE: Remember, I used to bring him to the studio and he sat in the control room when we were on the air, and every time he heard my voice he would bark, remember?

ACE: Yes, but I used to prefer to think he was laughing, which was more than our studio audience did.

JANE: Do you like that coat?

ACE: Yes, I always did, pure white.

JANE: No, I'm talking about my coat in this picture not Blackie's coat. Mine was black velvet. I think I look stunned.

ACE: Exactly. Now do you mind if we go on with the scripts?

MUSIC: MANHATTAN SERENADE
ACE: *Ladies and gentlemen, Easy Aces.*
MUSIC OUT

ACE: Since the subject this week is astrology, we have a couple of guest stars . . . Venus and Mars . . . Love and War . . . You know, the stuff that all's fair in. And when Jane started wrecking our home because I was born under the wrong sign of the zodiac, our guest stars must have had a good laugh.

BIZ REVERBERATING ECHO

MARS: (OFF) Hahahahahahahaha. What fools these mortals be!

VENUS: (OFF) (GIGGLES) Hahaha.

MARS: (OFF) Hahahahahahaha.

ECHO OUT

ACE: Oh before I forget, I've been asked to say that our guest stars appear through the courtesy of Daryl S. Zodiac, producer of *Night and Day*, and may currently be seen in your neighborhood sky . . . With a second feature, *Gemini's Agreement* . . . starring Celestial Holm . . . Directed by Frank Capricorn . . . Had enough? . . . Well, anyway, this all began one day last week when my boss, Mr. Norris, came into my office with some good news. When Mr. Norris has something to get off his chest, he talks like a stuffed shirt. Uses proverbs. This day the good news he had was about a raise in my salary.

NORRIS: Give credit where credit is due, I always say.

ACE: Well, thank you, Mr. Norris. I've waited a long time.

NORRIS: Patience is a virtue, I always say.

ACE: Well I've been patient, and now I'm rewarded.

NORRIS: Virtue is its *own reward*, I always say.

ACE: Well I've been virtue—ally without a raise for some time. Is this official, Mr. Norris?

NORRIS: It *will* be as soon as I sign this order to our cashier. (DOOR OPENS)

ACE: I have a pen right here, Mr.—

JANE: Hello, dear. (DOOR CLOSES)

ACE: Well, Jane, what brings you downtown this early?

JANE: Just fine. Hello, Mr. Norris. How are you?

NORRIS: I've been a little under the weather lately, Mrs. Ace.

JANE: Yes, isn't it?

ACE: Jane, Mr. Norris has just told me I'm gonna get a raise in salary.

JANE: Oh really, Mr. Norris.

NORRIS: Yes, just as soon as I sign this memorandum it'll become official.

ACE: The pen, Mr. Norris—here it is. (DOOR OPENS)

NORRIS: Oh yes, now I'll just—

MARGARET: Jonathan!

NORRIS: Oh hello, my dear.

MARGARET: Your secretary told me I'd find you here. I must speak to you immediately.

NORRIS: Come in, my dear—you know Mr. Ace, of course.

MARGARET: Good morning.

ACE: Hello, Mrs. Norris.

NORRIS: And, oh excuse me, Mrs. Ace, this is my wife.

MARGARET: How do you do, my dear.

JANE: Hello, Mrs. Norris.

NORRIS: I'll be finished in a minute, Margaret—I just have to sign this memoran—

MARGARET: Jonathan, no! That's why I came down here. You are not to sign anything today.

NORRIS: Oh no, Margaret, not again.

MARGARET: The moon is in Capricorn. You are not to sign anything for the next two weeks—

NORRIS: Oh, Margaret—

ACE: Moon in Capricorn?

MARGARET: I'm a firm believer in astrology, Mr. Ace. Everything Jonathan has, he owes to my astrological guidance.

ACE: But my raise—

NORRIS: Margaret, just this one little signature—

MARGARET: No, Jonathan.

NORRIS: Just my initials?

MARGARET: Jonathan will I have to hide your fountain pen again?

NORRIS: Oh, Margaret.

ACE: But my raise—

JANE: I don't get it, Mrs. Norris—what happened to the moon?

MARGARET: The moon is in Capricorn, my dear—a most unfavorable time for Jonathan to sign anything. He's a Gemini. I'm a Leo. What are you, my dear?

JANE: I'm a little mixed up.

ACE: But my raise—

MARGARET: Mrs. Ace, don't tell me you don't know about the influence of the stars on our lives.

JANE: All right.

ACE: My raise—

MARGARET: My dear, you should go at once to see Mr. Bush. He's my astrologer. I never make a move without him. He's simply wonderful. Twenty-two years ago he advised me to *marry* Jonathan.

NORRIS: Oh bushwa!

MARGARET: Jonathan, I won't have you casting disparaging remarks at Mr. Bush. You know he's responsible for your success in the advertising business. And wasn't it he who pointed out that since you were born in May, you were a Gemini, and I was born in August, so I'm a Leo—and May and August are most compatible months.

JANE: What am I, Mrs. Norris—I was born October 12th.

MARGARET: My dear you're a Libra.

JANE: I am? And who should I marry?

MARGARET: Mr. Bush can tell you that, my dear.

JANE: Dear, what are you?

ACE: I'm the goat. Now look, Jane, we're getting along fine—don't go looking for trouble. Aren't we happy?

JANE: Yes, that's right. Oh no, Mrs. Norris, I wouldn't pay any attention to that stuff—that's the silliest thing I ever heard. What's that man's name again?

MARGARET: Mr. Bush. He's so brilliant, dear—and so handsome.

JANE: Mr. Bush . . . He's really silly if he believes you can only marry somebody because they happen to be born in contemptible months—where's his office?

MARGARET: The Empire Building.

JANE: The Empire Building—honestly, Mrs. Norris, I don't see how you can believe anything like that . . . does he charge much?

MARGARET: Only five dollars for your chart.

JANE: Five dollars. Mrs. Norris, honestly I don't like to cast asparagus at the whole thing, but it sounds so silly—do you have to make an appointment?

MARGARET: No, just walk right in any time.

JANE: Well so long, dear, see you later.

ACE: Wait a minute—where you going?

JANE: I've got to find out why I was born.

MUSIC BRIDGE

ACE: So Jane went to see an astrologer.

VENUS: (OFF) (ON BIG ECHO) Giggles.

MARS: (OFF) (ON ECHO) Hahahahahahaha.

ECHO: OUT

ACE: What a studio audience they'd make. What laughs they had sitting up there on Mount Olympus looking down on this scene between Jane and Mr. Bush.

BUSH: Have a chair, madame.

JANE: Thank you. Mrs. Norris told me all about you, Mr. Bush.

BUSH: Oh, yes, Mrs. Norris.

JANE: She told me how you helped her and Mr. Norris. Can you help me that way?

BUSH: Are you interested in the signs of the Zodiac?

JANE: Oh no. I just wanta find out about my astrology.

BUSH: Yes, that's what I say. The signs of the Zodiac. We're all born under certain signs. Do you know which sign you were born under?

JANE: Uh—yes, I think I do remember—"Good to the last drop."

BUSH: What's that?

JANE: I remember there was a big sign over the house— it said "Good to the last drop."

BUSH: Good to the last—

JANE: It kept going off and on—I think it was one of those nylon signs.

BUSH: Mrs. uh—Ace—I'm afraid you don't understand. You see the signs I speak of are the signs of the Zodiac. They have their influence on our lives—and if you will give me some data, I will prepare a chart for you—first how old are you, Mrs. Ace?

JANE: Over twenty-one.

BUSH: Over twe—no, no, that won't do. I must have your exact age.

JANE: Oh but, Mr. Bush, there are certain things that are private, and this is it.

BUSH: But, madame, if I am to give you a reading—

JANE: I just couldn't indulge my age, Mr. Bush.

BUSH: Then how can I prepare a horoscope if I don't know the year and date of your birth?

JANE: Oh the year and date of my birth—why didn't you say so—October twelfth, 1915.

BUSH: Thank you, madame.

JANE: You're welcome. This is a nice office, Mr. Bush—I like that indiscreet lighting.

BUSH: Uh—yes. October twelfth makes you a Libra, my dear.

JANE: Yes, that's what Mrs. Norris said—now what should my husband be if I'm a Libra.

BUSH: Well there are certain people with whom you can be more harmonious. And they are people born under Sagittarius, Aquarius, Gemini, and Leo.

JANE: I used to know a fellow named Leo. But I never knew anybody named Sagittarius or—

BUSH: What is your husband's date of birth?

JANE: January fifteenth.

BUSH: Oh—a Capricorn.

JANE: Bad, huh.

BUSH: I wish you'd have met me before you married your husband.

JANE: Oh, Mr. Bush, this is so sudden.

BUSH: No, you don't understand—I mean I might have worked out something for you that could have protected such a union. And perhaps even now I can do as much for you. Tell me, do you remember the exact time of day you were born?

JANE: The exact time?

BUSH: Yes, it's rather important if you know it.

JANE: Well of course I was a little young at the time—what with all the excitement and everything—and the doctor and all that—

BUSH: Didn't your mother ever tell you?

JANE: You mean about the birds and bees?

BUSH: Yes. No. I mean the time of day—was it early morning —afternoon—late at night—surely your mother must have remembered that.

JANE: Oh yes, she was there at the time. But I don't think she ever told—

BUSH: Oh well, I'll do the best I can with the facts you've given me. Of course, it is unfortunate that your husband is a Capricorn and you a Libra—but I think I can manage to conjure up a protection for you against the bad influence of the sign of the Capricorn.

JANE: But how can you do that, Mr. Bush—I'm already married to him.

BUSH: I will make certain recommendations—and there are

certain charm rings, charm bracelets, and lockets which I will sell—which you should have—now suppose you let me make up your chart and you come back later in the day for my recommendations. Will you do that?

JANE: Oh sure, anything that'll make my husband and me happy again. Are you sure it'll work?

BUSH: Oh, of course. As a matter of fact, I have just finished an exact duplicate of your case, Mrs. Ace. Only it was the husband who came to see me. He's a Capricorn, and he was going to marry a beautiful young lady from Havana, who was born in October as you were.

JANE: Oh a Cuban Libra.

BUSH: Exactly. They are very happy now. Have no fear, Mrs. Ace, the stars will light the way.

JANE: Oh that's pretty . . . Has this astrology been going on long? I never paid much attention—

BUSH: The stars have had their influence over lovers since time itself. Lovers down through the ages have been guided by the stars. Take Romeo and Juliet.

JANE: Oh, but Romeo and Juliet didn't turn out so good. Didn't she take an overdose of sleeping tablets or something?

BUSH: Of course—and you know why?

JANE: Oh sure, I forgot—Romeo was a Montague, and Juliet was a Capricorn.

MUSIC BRIDGE

ACE: While Jane was at the office of Mr. Bush, setting astrology back one million light years, I was in my office wondering when Mrs. Norris would let the moon out of Capricorn. I couldn't get my raise without Norris's signature, and his wife had said he couldn't sign anything for the next two weeks—and in two weeks he might change his mind. I was sitting there thinking it was a pretty shabby trick of the moon to be in Capricorn at an important time like this (DOOR OPENS) when who should come in but Gemini himself. (DOOR CLOSES)

NORRIS: Mr. Ace, I'm terribly sorry about this.

ACE: Well, Mr. Norris, it *is* rather a shock almost to get a raise and then—

NORRIS: I know, I know. But it's Margaret. This has been going on for years. Don't sign this today. Don't make friends tomorrow. Beware of business relations *this* week. It's all too much for me. And too much is enough, I always say.

ACE: Well how about me—I was just about to get a raise and she—

NORRIS: Oh, your raise will be taken care of in time. I'll sign it when Margaret gives me the go-ahead. But I'm worried about you, Mr. Ace. Don't let this happen to you.

ACE: To me—what?

NORRIS: I heard Mrs. Ace say she was going to see this Mr. Bush—Mr. Ace, take a tip from me—stop her. Don't let her get mixed up with astrology. A hint to the wise is sufficient, I always say.

ACE: But nothing's gonna happen—I mean suppose she does go to see the man—

NORRIS: Please don't treat it so lightly, Mr. Ace. I've suffered this astrology thing for twenty-two years. It started with her first visit to Mr. Bush, and Mr. Bush now runs my life. I can't *open* a letter—I can't *answer* a letter—I can't take a business trip—I can't make a phone call, unless Mr. Bush sees it in the stars.

ACE: Great heavens.

NORRIS: I warn you, Mr. Ace. If your wife starts talking astrology to you, nip it in the bud—stop her before it's too late.

ACE: Well, thanks for the advice, Mr. Norris, but really—

NORRIS: This advice I am giving you, Mr. Ace, is the advice someone should have given me twenty-two years ago. I should have walked out of the house the first day she mentioned that man's name. And, Mr. Ace, I advise you to do the same now.

ACE: Walk out on my—well, let's don't turn this into a drama.

NORRIS: The play's the thing, I always say, Mr. Ace. You must take drastic action. A stitch in time saves nine, I always say. Promise me, Mr. Ace, for your own good if she starts quoting Mr. Bush to you, you will pack up and leave—that'll bring her to her senses.

ACE: Haha OK—if it'll make you happy, I promise, but I know my wife better than you do, and I'm sure you're getting upset over nothing.

NORRIS: Mighty oaks from little acorns grow, I always say, Mr. Ace.

ACE: That's your privilege.

NORRIS: It'll all begin very innocently, Mr. Ace. You won't

realize what's happening to you until it's too late. Little drops of water, little grains of sand, make a mighty ocean, and a lot of land, I always say.

ACE: You said a mouthful.

NORRIS: Mr. Ace if you had lived all these years in practically an observatory on top of Mount Wilson. If day after day you had to listen to "The sun is in Taurus, the sign of the bull, so Jonathan be cautious in money matters, but tomorrow the *moon* moves into Taurus, the sign of the bull, so, Jonathan, if you have an invention you want to invent, now is the time to invent it." That's what I've had to listen to for twenty-two years.

ACE: Sounds like a lot of Taurus to me.

MUSIC BRIDGE

ACE: With the signs of the Zodiac still ringing in my ears, I got home late that afternoon and there was no sign of Jane. But soon, she came bounding in.

ACE: Is that you, Jane?

JANE: (OFF) It's me, dear. I'm home.

ACE: And where have you been all afternoon?

JANE: Now just a minute, Capricorn.

ACE: You've been down to see Mr. Bush.

JANE: A very good question. And I'll explain everything that happened.

ACE: I wish you would.

JANE: Well, to make a long story—

ACE: Don't make a long story—just get to the point and then we'll forget it.

JANE: Now just a minute, dear, you're the one who wrecked our marriage.

ACE: Wrecked our marriage?

JANE: You're the one who was born January fifteenth, not me.

ACE: Well, I'm sorry I picked that day, Jane—

JANE: And who do you think is to blame?

ACE: Me, I suppose.

JANE: You—you Capricorn.

ACE: No names, please.

JANE: It's a good thing I went to Mr. Bush. He told me we can't get along together.

ACE: Well if we can't get along, I guess I'll just move out.

JANE: Oh no you don't have to move out. Mr. Bush protected me against you.

ACE: You sure need protection.

JANE: A very good question. And here's how we do it. See this ring and this bracelet I'm wearing? They're engraved—they say Libra. And here's another ring and bracelet that say Capricorn.

ACE: Where did you get all this junk?

JANE: Junk—junk—

ACE: Sorry, we haven't anything today lately.

JANE: I'll have you understand these charms cost twenty-five cents apiece. Now, you're gonna wear this ring and

this bracelet—come on, let's put on the bracelet, first—
come on, dear, make a wrist.

ACE: You mean to say our marriage depends on a dollar's
worth of junk jewelry?

JANE: A dollar ten—tax, you know.

ACE: Our marriage license cost two dollars.

JANE: We save ninety cents right there. Come on, dear, put it
on.

ACE: Jane, this is the end. I'm gonna nip this thing in the
bud. This house is not gonna be turned into a planetar-
ium. I'm leaving.

JANE: Leaving—where you going?

ACE: Oh, I don't know—home to Father, I guess.

MUSIC BRIDGE

ACE: So I followed through with Mr. Norris's advice and
left home. It was the first free night I'd had in years. I
was on the town. Had some chop suey—then I bowled a
couple of games—did pretty good—broke a hundred—
bought a candy apple on a stick—did pretty good there,
too—broke a porcelain jacket on my tooth—went to a news-
reel theater—watched the electric signs on Times Square
—and then went over, got a room at the YMCA—
Young Men's Capricorn Association. When I got to the
office the next morning I thought sure there would be
some word from Jane . . . Nothing . . . I called home
and got no answer. I found out later she had gone over
to Mrs. Norris's home for further instructions.

JANE: (WORRIED) What do I do now, Mrs. Norris?

MARGARET: You mean he's left you?

JANE: He walked out on me last night and didn't come home. There have been nights when he stayed out late—but not to come home at all—that's the latest he's *ever* stayed out.

MARGARET: Well, my dear, that's what a Libra can expect from a Capricorn.

JANE: But, Mrs. Norris, he's been a Capricorn all these years, and a rather nice Capricorn too. Maybe I made a mistake starting all this fuss about—

MARGARET: Nonsense, my dear. I have complete confidence in Mr. Bush. And don't you worry about your husband's leaving you. I'll phone Jonathan at the office right now and he'll speak to that husband of yours and give him a piece of my mind.

JANE: Oh I wish you would, Mrs. Norris. Would you?
(PHONE UP AND DIALS)

MARGARET: Of course, my dear. Meanwhile you're going to live here with us.

JANE: Because you have no idea what a lonesome feeling it is to look across the breakfast table in the morning and not see that newspaper staring me in the face—even if he is only a Capricorn.

MUSIC BRIDGE

ACE: How do you like that—isn't that just like a woman, spilling all her personal troubles to the first outsider that comes along? You don't catch men doing that. I sat in my office, suffering silently. That's the way Mr. Norris found me when he came into my office.

NORRIS: Good morning, Mr. Ace.

ACE: Is it? It isn't to me. I did what you told me to last night. I left home. I spent an uncomfortable night at the YMCA—I lost the porcelain jacket off my tooth—I got up this morning with chop suey on my tie, and went to the Automat for breakfast and if you think it's fun sitting at a breakfast table reading a newspaper with nobody to interrupt you, you're mistaken. She may be a Libra, but she's not a bad little Libra, as Libras go. I think I made a mistake starting all this fuss over—

NORRIS: Nonsense. You did the right thing. Be firm. Rock of Gibraltar, assert yourself. Some say you'll thank me for this. (PHONE RINGS)

ACE: Hello.

MARGARET: (FILTER) This is Mrs. Norris, I want to speak to my husband.

ACE: Uh—just a minute. It's Mrs. Norris.

NORRIS: Oh what does she want now. Hello, Margaret.

MARGARET: Jonathan, I want you to speak to Mr. Ace and tell him he's got to go home to his wife.

NORRIS: But Margaret this is no affair of ours—

MARGARET: Jonathan, do you hear me?

NORRIS: But if Mr. Ace leaves his wife, I have no reason to—

MARGARET: Jonathan, you heard what I said.

ACE: Be firm, Mr. Norris.

MARGARET: If you don't speak to him, I'll never speak to *you* again.

ACE: Assert yourself.

MARGARET: Is what I'm saying penetrating that thick head of yours?

ACE: Rock of Gibraltar.

MARGARET: Well, Jonathan, are you going to do as I tell you? . . . (PAUSE)

NORRIS: No, Margaret.

MARGARET: What?

NORRIS: I think Mr. Ace did the wise thing. I stand behind him, hook, line and sinker.

ACE: Look—sinker—don't get me into this—

MARGARET: Jonathan Norris, this is the end. I will send your things to your office. You are not to set foot in this house again. I'll protect this woman from her husband —she stays with me until both of you come to your senses. Goodbye. (CLICK)

NORRIS: Yes, Marg—*Goodbye.* (HANGS UP WITH A BANG) Well, Mr. Ace—I asserted myself. I was firm—Rock of Gibraltar—uh, what do I do now?

ACE: What do you do—you move into the YMCA with me. We'll go on the town tonight—how are you on candy apples?

MUSIC BRIDGE

ACE: Well, that night Mr. Norris and I had chop suey. He

doesn't bowl so we each bought a candy apple. I broke another porcelain jacket. By the time Mr. Norris had disengaged his upper plate from the candy apple, he was exhausted, so we went home . . . Home . . . What is home without a woman's touch? . . . A gin rummy game, natch.

NORRIS: That's gin, Mr. Ace—how could you throw me the jack of clubs when I picked your ten of clubs?

ACE: Oh I didn't remember—I've been eating too many of these chocolates—I gotta cut it out—my waist line's getting to be abominable.

MUSIC CHORD

ACE: Meanwhile over at Mrs. Norris's home:

MARGARET: That's gin, my dear—how could you throw me the five of hearts when I picked your six of hearts?

JANE: Oh, I didn't remember. I was thinking maybe he might be eating too many of those chocolates. He's gotta cut it out. His waist line's getting abdominal.

MARGARET: Oh, stop worrying about your husband. He'll be all right. I just hope Jonathan doesn't forget to take his vitamin pill.

JANE: If he goes home, I hope he knows there's some cold chicken in the refrigerator—he always likes a midnight smack.

MARGARET: I hope he doesn't give Jonathan any. I've got him on a very rigid diet.

JANE: Maybe you oughta call him up and tell him not to eat any.

MARGARET: I should say I won't. But if it'll ease your mind I will. (PHONE UP AND DIAL)

JANE: Yes, call him up.

MARGARET: He needs more care than a child. Out of my sight for one night and he's eating cold chicken and not taking his vitamin pills.

JANE: I should have hidden those chocolates so he couldn't find 'em.

ACE: (FILTER) Hello.

MARGARET: Mr. Ace, this is Mrs. Norris—may I speak to Mr. Norris?

ACE: Whatsa matter—anything wrong—is Jane all right?

MARGARET: She's perfectly all right—do you wish to speak to her?

ACE: Yes, I'd like to.

MARGARET: Just a minute—your husband wants to speak to you.

JANE: Oh, finally.

MARGARET: But wait just a minute, my dear—I don't think you should.

JANE: But I miss him—

MARGARET: You've got to teach him a lesson—he's weakening. Be firm—assert yourself—Rock of Gibralter. Be a Libra!

JANE: But let me just say—

MARGARET: Hello, Mr. Ace. Mrs. Ace refuses to speak to you. Let me talk to Mr. Norris.

ACE: Oh, is that so? Well, Mr. Norris refuses to speak to you.

MARGARET: He does? Oh, he does. Well, give him this message. He's not to eat any of that cold chicken in your refrigerator.

ACE: OK, I'll tell him.

JANE: But I wanta tell my husband about the chocolates.

MARGARET: Oh yes, Mrs. Ace has a message for you.

ACE: Well, tell her to give it to Mr. Norris, I'll put him on.

MARGARET: Here you are, my dear—you can speak to Jonathan.

NORRIS: Hello.

JANE: Hello Mr. Norris. How is he?

NORRIS: He's fine. What's the message you have for him?

JANE: Message? Oh yes. Tell him not to eat too many of those chocolates.

NORRIS: Thank you. I'll tell him. Oh, Mrs. Ace—how is Margaret?

JANE: Oh she's fair to meddling.

NORRIS: Still at it, huh.

MARGARET: Oh I forgot about the vitamin pill.

JANE: Mrs. Norris has another message for you, Mr. Norris.

NORRIS: Just a minute—I'll put Mr. Ace on.

JANE: He's putting my husband on—here you talk to him— but I'll peek into the receiver with one ear.

ACE: Hello.

MARGARET: Mr. Ace, tell Jonathan he's not to forget his vitamin pill.

ACE: Very well, I'll tell him.

JANE: Hello, dear.

ACE: Wait a minute—who's got the ball—who's this message for?

JANE: It's me, dear. Are you all right?

ACE: Don't worry about me—how you making out?

JANE: Me either.

ACE: Well you started this. It's the most ridiculous thing—

JANE: Just because I wanted to find out about astrology?

ACE: I don't mind astrology—if you wanta go in for it—but not the way you did—I'm willing to meet you halfway.

JANE: You will, dear? All right—we're at 86th Street, and you're at 76th—we'll meet you halfway—on the corner of 81st. I'll bring Mrs. Norris with me.

ACE: OK, I'll bring a friend for her.

MUSIC BRIDGE

ACE: And so it came to pass that on this balmy May evening two couples met on the corner of 81st Street and Fifth Avenue. I wish you could have been there to see this happy reunion:

MARGARET: I certainly will not speak to him unless he speaks to me first.

ACE: Well, you started the whole thing.

JANE: Are you all right, dear?

NORRIS: You and that phony Mr. Bush.

MARGARET: Don't you call him phony.

JANE: Did you miss me, dear?

ACE: And you gypped me out of a raise besides breaking up my home.

MARGARET: You broke up your own home when you left your wife.

NORRIS: You stay out of other people's affairs, Margaret.

JANE: You look tired, dear.

ALL THREE: Jonathan Norris I'll never forgive you . . . You've got to stop meddling in other people's lives . . . You and your Capricorns and Libras—

COP: Hey—come on here—break it up—what's going on here—pipe down.

JANE: Oh hello, policeman.

COP: What's going on here—you people got a permit to hold a meeting?

NORRIS: Oh no, officer, we're not holding a meeting—

ACE: No sir, we're just having a family dispute—

JANE: We're all married.

COP: Married? Now is that a nice way for married folks to act? On a beautiful balmy spring night like this? It's spring folks—look at that sky up there—look at all those beautiful stars up there.

ACE: Don't start with those stars again—

COP: Look at 'em up there—Venus and Mars—

ACE: Come on, Jane—let's go home—good night, Mr. Norris.

NORRIS: Good night.

JANE: Good night, Mrs. Norris.

MARGARET: Good night, my dear—come along Jonathan.

COP: Good night, folks—

ALL: Good night, officer.

COP: Yes, there's nothing like those stars up there to make people happy.

VENUS: (ON ECHO) Giggles.

MARS: (ECHO) Hahahahahahahaha.

MUSIC PLAYOFF

JANE GOES INTO THE CHRISTMAS
CARD BUSINESS

ACE: OK on that script, co-author?

JANE: Yes, and you know why? Because it's true. Remember, we really had a big argument about that? It shows that truth is stranger than friction. I believe in the stars.

ACE: Who was it who said "The fault, dear Brutus, is not in our stars, but in ourselves, that we are underlings?"

JANE: Not me! All I said was I believe in the stars and if you weren't so obstinate, you would change your birthdate so we could be more combatable.

ACE: I think we're doing very well in that department.

JANE: That has all the ear muffs of a dirty dig.

ACE: Speaking of dirty, these scripts are pretty messy. Don't you think you can launder them or iron out the wrinkles or something?

JANE: Now just a minute, my tar-feathered friend, you know what we decided when our maid left us.

Well, I better go into the dirty details of how we lost our maid some time ago. After a happy association with us for twenty years, she came and asked me for a cut in salary. After some probing, it turned out that she had reached the time when she could get old-age money from the government, only if she earned no more than $1200 a year. If she didn't get the cut she would go on strike. This was not a radio script, although it could have been.

I tried to explain that she wouldn't collect enough to make up the difference. But she insisted it was the patriotic thing to do. The government was her shepherd and she would not want.

A year later she was back with another deal. She had talked to some other maids, who were getting extra money from their employers. "*Sous la table*," she said.

"*Non, non, sur la table!*" I replied. I was not going to be a party to any shenanigans like that. "I'm as patriotic as you are," I said. So she left us in high dudgeon. Which was a double-deck bus that ran all the way down to where she lived in low dudgeon.

Jane interviewed several other maids, but the references were not good; Jane's references, not the maids'. Especially that part about Jane's having her breakfast at 7 o'clock. So for two years we have been without the services of a maid.

It was then that a transformation came over the head of our house. She became chairman of the board. She called a meeting. She was chairman, and I was bored. I have here a transcript of the minutes of that meeting, not in complete detail. You may guess why from the length of her opening statement:

"Dear," she said, "we are going to have to be our own maids. It's up to us to keep this apartment spic and spat. Neatness is next to godliness."

"I think that's cleanliness," I corrected.

"All right," she continued, "neatness is next to cleanliness. I'm tired of having this baffle of wits with maids. As far as I'm concerned they can all go hire a kite. They're all alike. Birds of a father flock together, as the saying goes. What are we going to do, just sit here like a couple of simonized twins? No, sir. Not us. You'll be the maid for your den and half of the living room, and I'll be vice-versa. And if I have to, I can do the cooking. I can strangle an egg, I can TV a dinner, and can make instant coffee in fifteen minutes or less. When it comes to housekeeping I'm no shrieking violet. When I was in high school, I took domestic silence for two years."

"Why don't you practice it?"

"I will. We both will."

"Do I get paid a maid's salary?"

"No, and so will I. Think of the money we'll save."

"Sounds like a get-rich-quick scheme."

"What's the matter with getting rich quick? Why drag it out? The quicker the faster."

The telephone rang. "You better answer it, dear. It may be the phone," she said. So I answered it. It was the phone.

"Hello . . . No, this is the maid . . . OK, hold it. I'll pick it up on the way down." It was the doorman telling me there was a special delivery letter.

"Dear," she said, "I don't think you ought to say 'This is the maid.' You better say 'This is the butler.' Now let's get busy and get this apartment neat. This is our home. Remember, be it ever so hovel, there's no place like home."

At the end of the day she came to my side of the apartment for inspection. I didn't make it.

"*Look* at that wastebasket! Three pieces of paper on the floor. You missed the basket three times," she scolded.

"I never claimed to be a Harlem Globe Trotter," I replied, picking up the missed shots. I lost six points right there.

As the first week went on, I lost others. The big one was when I had to send out my laundry. This had been part of our maid's routine. I was told to empty the hamper and make two lists. "One for them," she said, "and vice-versa." I gathered up the laundry and neatly typed two lists.

"What's this?" she said. "Thirteen socks?"

"That's right. One of the socks had a big hole in the toe. I threw it away. Now when one of my other socks has a hole in it, I'll throw that one away and match the other with the one sock that I'm sending today, which will make an even pair."

"How's that again?"

"Look, just let it go. I'm sending thirteen socks."

"You can't do that. What will they think?"

"What will who think?"

"Dear, I have one question I want to ask you. I have a sister who lives in St. Louis."

"That is not a question."

"Oh. Well, do I have a sister who lives in St. Louis?"

"Yes, you do."

"Well, when her maid left them, she and her husband became the maids, and if they can do it, so can we. And if I'm wrong, I'm not far from it."

"Well, I've been pitching in and doing my part."

"Not all of it. You're not doing well in dusting. I noticed the top of your dresser. Dusting doesn't mean running your finger over your dust and writing 'Help!'"

"Well, I'm new at it," I said. "This is something our maid used to do."

"Don't mention her name to me."

"I didn't."

"When I think of all the years she was here and all my clothes I gave her."

"Your clothes? You're a size six and she must have been a sixteen."

"The gloves fit her."

"Look, let's forget about her—let's sweep all that under the rug."

"That's another thing, she . . ."

"I'm sorry I said that. But you have to admit that as a maid she was rather deft."

"Oh no, she wasn't. She heard what she wanted to hear."

"Look, Jane, she was loyal—she came to work on time every morning."

"How about that morning she was seventy-five minutes late."

"Seventy-five min . . ."

"Yes, sir. Three-quarters of an hour. And the week after that she didn't show up for two days."

"She explained it; she was sick."

"She had intentional flu, she told us. You don't get well in two days from that. Then out of a clean sky she ups and outs. People just don't want to work."

"Well, you can hardly blame them. When they reach that age, they get social security, they feel they deserve a rest— got it coming to them. The world is their oyster."

"I know what you mean—you don't have to draw any blue points for me. It's just that I feel sad about the way she did it. She was like one of the family. Like an old family Airedale. Well, there's no use crying over spoiled milk. I just wanted to get it all out of my cistern. Now let's get to work cleaning up here."

"I thought I'd go over to the office first and write a . . ."

"Not before you hang up all your clothes, put those shoes away, put that shirt in the laundry, and dust your Venetians."

"Yes, boss, and tote that barge and lift that bale?"

"Listen, dear, there's a time to joke and a time not. An this is it. Instead of complaining just think of the money we'll save by not having a maid. We'll save thousands."

"Are you talking dollars?"

"I'm certainly not talking cents."

"I pass."

"And what we'll save on shopping goes without saying. She spent money like a drunken tailor."

"Well, the cost of living is getting higher all the time."

"And you know why it is? Because prices are getting higher."

"Yes, the old question of the chicken and the egg."

"Yes, and butter too. Everything's high. But she bought so much at a time. I buy less, so it doesn't cost so much. Well, let's get to work. Start hanging up those clothes of yours, while I clean my half of this hall mirror. There's a big black spot on it, look at it."

"No, Jane, there's a smudge on your forehead."

"Oh, yes. Well, you pick up your clothes while I go clean my forehead."

And that's the way it's been going for some time. She has been playing Craig's Wife to my Arthur Treacher. And somehow, despite all the scrambled dialogue, this hour of our travail has brought a new warmth to our relationship. No butler and maid can publicly make that statement. So much for reminiscing.

ACE: This script looks like it might read well, Jane. It's about the day you decided to go into business for yourself—selling Christmas cards.

MUSIC: MANHATTAN SERENADE
ACE: *Ladies and gentlemen, Easy Aces.*
MUSIC OUT

ACE: Once upon a time there was a happy couple who never argued about money. If the people next door bought a big new car, but she had to go on the subway, she never complained . . . If on her birthday he just gave

her a kiss instead of an expensive present, it was all right
with her . . . If he wanted to go to a neighborhood movie
instead of an expensive Broadway show, she never ob-
jected . . . Then they were married. And we've been
arguing about money ever since.

JANE: Dear, in all the years we've been married, I never did
know exactly how much money you make.

ACE: Let's keep it that way, shall we?

JANE: No, we won't. Because I can't get along on the money
you give me. And I don't know how much more to ask
you for.

ACE: Well, what is it that you haven't got, that you need?

JANE: Oh—they're too humorous to mention. I don't mean to
say that we're living in squandor—

ACE: Squandor—yes—

JANE: But it's just that little things come up around the
house, and I just can't make both ends neat. You know
what I think we're trying to do, dear?

ACE: What?

JANE: We're trying to live within our income.

ACE: Shame on us.

JANE: Exactly. Now tell me, dear, how much money do you
make?

ACE: I have a drawing account of fifty-two hundred a year.

JANE: Fifty-two hundred a year—is that all?

ACE: Do you know many people who make five thousand
a year?

JANE: Oh *five* thousand two hundred—why didn't you say so?

ACE: Trying to hold out on you.

JANE: Now let me see—five thousand two hundred a year—fifty-two weeks a year—that's ten dollars a wee—no.

ACE: No.

JANE: I forgot to carry the cider.

ACE: That's what makes it hard. But then of course I get a Christmas bonus.

JANE: When do you get that?

ACE: Decoration Day.

JANE: Wait a minute—Christmas—that gives me an idea. What do you think if I made some extra money selling Christmas cards?

ACE: In *May*, Jane?

JANE: What of it? May, Jane, July, August, the summer's over—Labor Day, October, my birthday, November, Thanksgiving, and boom—it's Christmas.

ACE: I think I'll go down and shake up the furnace.

JANE: All I have to do is get the cards, and some paint, take the orders and make money. There must be a big profit in Christmas cards, doesn't it to you, dear?

ACE: I don't know what the profit is, but you're not—

JANE: Oh sure you know what profit is—profit and loss—

ACE: Yes, I know—

JANE: Profit is the money you make and loss is the money you don't.

ACE: Loss is the money you—

JANE: But why think about loss? What have I got to lose? Just two things—the cost of the cards, the cost of the paint, and my time.

ACE: Just those two—

JANE: Yes sir, this is it. I can get rich. The only way to get rich is to make money.

ACE: Fine way to get rich—selling Christmas greetings.

JANE: I can't miss—it's in the cards.

MUSIC BRIDGE: WHITE CHRISTMAS

ACE: (HUMS) Beautiful song, isn't it? Especially in summertime. It's around the middle of December that it gets monotonous—when your radio bangs it at you all day long—or Bings it at you. Well, let me see—it was the next day around noon—when I had gone out to lunch—that Jane came down to my office in the advertising firm of Dutton, Sutton, Mutton and Norris, and took my secretary, Miss Anderson, into the Christmas card business as a partner. She couldn't have made a wiser choice. Miss Anderson is sharp as a marble. Witness this business conference:

JANE: And I thought we could use your desk as our office, Sally, and sell our Christmas cards right from here. Do you wanta be a partner?

ANDERSON: Christmas cards in May, Jane?

JANE: Oh what of it—May, Jane, July August, and the summer's over. Labor Day, October, my birthday, November, Thanksgiving and boom—it's Christmas.

ANDERSON: Well, when you put it that way, Jane—but I don't know much about business—I have my hands full taking dictation here and—

JANE: All we have to do is get some cards—raw cards—and we take orders from people and paint on the cards whatever they want.

ANDERSON: But can you paint Christmas cards, Jane? I don't think I can.

JANE: Well what's hard about that? Sure you can—a little snow, a little mistletoe, and Merry Christmas.

ANDERSON: Yes, but how about church windows? People like church windows on Christmas cards. I do. They're hard to paint.

JANE: Not if you leave 'em open . . . Stop being so practical. All we have to do is buy some raw cards, and some paint, and start some advertising.

ANDERSON: But Jane that's gonna take money. I haven't any money.

JANE: Who's got money? If I had money do you think I'd be going into business?

ANDERSON: Well how do you get the cards and the paint and the advertising? That takes money.

JANE: We charge it.

ANDERSON: Charge it to who?

JANE: Well we charge it to—oh Sally, I think that should be charge it "to whom."

ANDERSON: Oh yes.

JANE: To is a proposition or something, and you have to say whom. No offense of course.

ANDERSON: Oh no, that's all right, Jane.

JANE: You're welcome—now uh—what was the question again?

ANDERSON: Charge it to whom? You've got to pay for the cards and all that stuff.

JANE: Oh no, you've got the cards before the horse. First we sell 'em and the money we have left over is the profit.

ANDERSON: But suppose we don't have any money left over.

JANE: Well, that's the money they call a loss.

ANDERSON: What do we do with that?

JANE: There isn't much you can do with it—pay our bills and things like that. For the cards and the paint and the advertising—and that's where you come in, Sally. They use a lot of cards and paint around the office here—where do you order it from?

ANDERSON: All our stationery comes from the Zenith Printing Company and our paint from the Royal Paint Company—

JANE: Well OK, partner, let's get busy—call 'em up—let's order the stuff. Get 'em on the phone—you've gotta *do* something if you're gonna make all this money. What do you think this is—Christmas?

MUSIC BRIDGE: JINGLE BELLS

ACE: And this is how I was taken for a sleigh ride in a one horse open business. First they called the printer:

ANDERSON: Hello, Mr. O'Brien, this is Miss Anderson—Mr. Ace's secretary.

PRINTER: (VERY IRISH) (FILTER) Oh yes, Miss Anderson, and how's Mr. Ace?

ANDERSON: He's OK, if you like, Mr. Ace. But Mrs. Ace wants to speak to you, Mr. O'Brien.

JANE: Gimme, Sally.

PRINTER: Mrs. Ace? Well I've never met the lady.

JANE: Hello, Mr. O'Brien, this is Mrs. Ace. I want to order some raw cards to make some Christmas cards.

PRINTER: Christmas cards in May?

JANE: Another one. What of it? May Jane July and August—oh I'm not going through that again—do you have the cards, Mr. O'Brien?

PRINTER: Sure—how many do you want—a gross?

JANE: A gross? How many is that about?

PRINTER: A dozen dozen—is that too many?

JANE: No, a dozen dozen doesn't seem too many, does it, Sally?

ANDERSON: No, a dozen dozen doesn't seem too many.

JANE: OK, Mr. O'Brien—a gross.

PRINTER: OK—and charge 'em to Dutton, Sutton, Mutton and Norris, I suppose?"

JANE: Well—

PRINTER: Thank you, Mrs. Ace. Goodbye.

JINGLE BELLS . . . SHORT

ACE: Then they called the paint company.

JANE: I'd like to order some paint—mostly red and green—
it's for painting some Christmas cards.

PAINTER COMPANY: (FILTER) Christmas cards in May?

JANE: What of it? Why does everybody say in May? This is
getting jerksome. Is this a democracy or isn't it?

JINGLE BELLS . . . SHORT

ACE: After charging the paint supplies to me, they called a
little radio station to buy some advertising time:

JANE: And so I want to advertise some Christmas cards for
sale . . . (PAUSE) Well, what of it?

RADIOMAN: (FILTER) I didn't say anything.

JANE: Oh I thought you were gonna say "in May?" Well do
you think you can find a nice place on your radio station
for our little advertisement?

RADIOMAN: I may.

JANE: There's that May again. What of it—May—Jane—July—

MUSIC BRIDGE: JINGLE BELLS

ACE: So the two card sharps charged everything to me and I
didn't know a thing about it. The radio station sent
them a complicated contract. There was a thirteen-week
clause, a non-cancelable clause, and a clause charging
everything to me. The Santa Clause. . . . Now we fade—

it's a week later—after dinner at home. I'm sitting there reading the baseball scores while Jane and Miss Anderson are getting out Christmas cards . . . There's a parlay for you . . . Over the corner of my newspaper, I overhear this choice bit of dialogue:

ANDERSON: Whew! Let's rest a while, Jane.

JANE: Me too. Doesn't it get hot painting all this snow?

ANDERSON: I'm surprised it stays on in this weather. Haha.

JANE: Haha that's pretty good—surprised it stays on. Dear, did you hear—oh he's reading the paper.

ANDERSON: Jane I'm getting kinda worried—we haven't had one order for cards.

JANE: Well, my goodness, Sally, we've only advertised one week—home wasn't built in a day. But when they start to call, we'll be ready for 'em. We've got forty cards painted—we're making very good headwork.

ANDERSON: Maybe we started this business a little too early. It's seven months till Christmas. Could it be we're a little premature?

JANE: Please, Sally, not in front of him.

ANDERSON: No, I mean maybe we should have taken a holiday a little closer. Maybe Thanksgiving. We could change the cards, you know.

JANE: Yeh, these reindeer do look a little like turkeys; but Sally, we can't change horses in mid-spring.

ANDERSON: Are you sure, Jane, you advertised the right phone number?

JANE: Sure, I'm sure. I gave both telephone numbers—the

house, and the office. Don't worry so much, Sally. It's a little slow now, but business'll pick up by creeps and bounds. (PHONE UP AND DIAL) We'll be selling Christmas cards like a horse on fire before you even—dear—what are you doing?

ACE: What? I'm just calling up the drugstore to get some cigars.

JANE: Put that phone down. That's a business phone.

ACE: Business phone—I need some cigars.

JANE: Somebody might be trying to put in an order and all that business goes up in smoke. If you want cigars why don't you walk up to the corner and get some.

ACE: Isn't that awful. All right I'll go up to the corner.

JANE: Thanks dear. All right, Sally, let's get back to work— now be careful—not too much snow—you've got snow all over these things, and I—dear, haven't you gone yet? What are you looking for?

ACE: My ear muffs and goulashes.

MUSIC BRIDGE: WINTER WONDERLAND

ACE: As I mushed out of our apartment and down the corridor, I suddenly got a brilliant idea. I stopped short. "Whoa prancer—whoa dancer—whoa Martha Graham." I pulled the sled up in front of the one and a half room igloo of our next door neighbor, Ken Roberts—he's the radio announcer.

KEN: Well, come in, Mr. Ace—where's Jane?

ACE: Jane is busy getting out Christmas cards.

KEN: Christmas cards in May?

ACE: What of it? May, June, July, Saratoga, September, Bowie, November, Santa Anita and boom it's Christmas. May I use your phone, Ken?

KEN: Sure—whatsa matter, your phone out of order?

ACE: No it's a business phone—Jane and her cousin, Miss Anderson, have gone into the Christmas card business and they haven't had any orders yet, so I thought I'd help 'em out.

KEN: Oh, I get it—go ahead use the phone.

ACE: I hate to bother you.

KEN: Oh, it's quite all right. Anytime. Make your call.

ACE: Thank you. (COIN DROPS IN PHONE, AND DIALS)

KEN: Do you think she'll recognize your voice?

ACE: (WESTERN DRAWL) Oh, I don't think so, pardner.

KEN: Hey, that's good. Ever thought of going on the radio, Mr. Ace?

ACE: Where I hail from we call that rodeo, son.

JANE: (FILTER) Hello.

ACE: Hello there!

JANE: Yes? Who are you calling, please?

ACE: I understand you're sellin' Christmas cards, ma'am.

JANE: Christmas cards—yes, sir—just a minute, sir—pencil, Sally—yes, sir—what can I do for you, sir?

ACE: Well sir, how much are they, ma'am?

JANE: Well we have different prices—depends on how many you want to buy—the more you buy the cheaper it is— like we charge five dollars for one dozen, but if you buy two dozen, we charge seven fifty—the more you buy the less they are. How many did you want, sir?

ACE: One.

JANE: One?

ACE: One, ma'am.

JANE: One dozen, you mean?

ACE: No ma'am, just one card.

JANE: Just one card—one? The first number in the alphabet?

ACE: Uh—yes, that's right ma'am—

JANE: Well—how about all your friends?

ACE: I don't have any friends, ma'am—just my horse on the lone prairie . . . How much would one card be, ma'am?

JANE: Well, I don't know exactly—

ACE: What kind of business you runnin' that you don't know the prices?

JANE: Oh, I know the prices for a dozen or two dozen and so so and so so—but we just haven't figured how much one would be.

ACE: We? Who's we, gal?

JANE: My partner and I.

ACE: Howdy, partner.

JANE: Howdy . . . What did you say your name was?

ACE: My name's Austin Dallas—from Fort Worth, ma'am. My friends call me Cheyenne.

JANE: Howdy.

ACE: Howdy, pardner. Wanta have something special on my Christmas card.

JANE: Well, we have some with snow—some with holly—and some with open church windows.

ACE: No cactus?

JANE: Cactus in snow? I never heard of that.

ACE: I never heard of Christmas cards in May.

JANE: Oh, you too . . .

ACE: What's that, gal?

JANE: Nothing. Well if you want cactus, we'll give you cactus. But you'll have to call me back and I'll let you know how much one'll cost. Call me back in about an hour.

ACE: Adios, amigo. Buenos pancho, rancho grande.

JANE: Uh—yippee.

MUSIC BRIDGE: HOME ON THE RANGE

ACE: Well, strangers, after makin' that telephone call, I moseyed on over to my own corral, dusted the sagebrush off my chaps, unbowed my legs and walked in. There they were—two empty saddles . . . Messin' around with old paint—and new Christmas cards.

JANE: Dear, you missed it—we just had an order.

ACE: Really, Jane?

ANDERSON: Some order—one Christmas card.

JANE: Sally, I know that's about the least anybody can order, but it's a good start. Now all we have to figure out is how much to charge him.

ACE: Who is he, Jane?

JANE: I don't know—sounds like a cowboy or something— talked with a Western drool. And instead of mistletoe, he wants cactuses on the card.

ACE: Cacti, Jane.

JANE: Beg pardon?

ACE: The plural of cactus is cacti.

JANE: Oh, I didn't know that, dear. Thanks.

ACE: You're welcome, Jane—glad to be of service—call me any time—I'm in the book.

ANDERSON: Well, so much for grammar, how about arithmetic, Jane—how much are we gonna charge him?

JANE: Well that's the fly in the oatmeal. Now let's figure it out—the more you buy, the less it is, is that right?

ANDERSON: That's right, Jane.

JANE: Then the less you buy, the more it is. Did I say that right?

ANDERSON: I think so.

JANE: Wait—I'll say that over again. Now listen carefully.

ACE: I'm listening.

JANE: Not you, dear. Now stop that.

ACE: What did I do?

JANE: I don't like that tone in your eye. We're talking business. We've gotta figure this out before he calls back. Please stay out of it.

ACE: Well, I can see I'm not wanted around here—I think I'll go over and visit with Ken Roberts for a while.

JANE: Yes you do that, dear—wait a minute—you're not going visiting looking like that, are you? Button up your shirt collar, and put on your necktus.

ACE: Necktus?

JANE: Cactus, cacti—necktus, necktie.

MUSIC BRIDGE

ACE: Ken, do you remember that name I used before?

KEN: Somewhere in Texas wasn't it?

ACE: Oh yeh—uh—Dallas, uh—

JANE: (FILTER) Hello.

ACE: (WESTERN) Hello there, ma'am.

JANE: Hello there.

ACE: Have you figured out how much that Christmas card is gonna cost me?

JANE: My partner and I are just figuring it out.

ACE: Howdy, pardner.

JANE: Howdy. Well, here's the way we figured it out. The more you buy, the less you pay. So the less you pay the more you buy. Did I say that right?

ACE: No, I don't think so, ma'am.

JANE: No, I wasn't asking you did I say that right. I was asking my partner did I say that right.

ACE: Howdy, pardner.

JANE: Howdy. Just a minute. I'll ask her again. Uh—hold your horse.

ACE: Whoa, there . . .

KEN: What did she say?

ACE: She's asking Miss Anderson. They're trying to figure out just how much—

JANE: Hello.

ACE: Hello there, pardner.

JANE: Uh—hello there, pardner. Well, this is the way we figured it out. We can't break a dozen, so we'll sell you a dozen for five dollars. And you can use one if you want to, or all of 'em. That's our blackbottom price.

ACE: But I can't use a dozen, ma'am. Nobody to send 'em to.

JANE: Well, my advice to you is to be friendlier between now and Christmas.

ACE: I'll just stick to my old horse.

JANE: Aren't you married?

ACE: Gosh no, ma'am.

JANE: Well, would you like to meet a nice young lady, who is a very good secretary, and owns half interest in a Christmas card business, and is willing to travel west?

ACE: I'll just stick to my horse. I don't mind paying five

dollars, ma'am but I want something pretty good for my money. Something new, something novel. Rustle up something for me and I'll call you later, ma'am.

JANE: All right—call me back in half an hour.

ACE: I'll do that, ma'am— (HANGS UP)

KEN: They still haven't caught on?

ACE: No, Ken, but I'm afraid they might—if I keep walking out everytime the call comes through—so you call while I'm over there. Can you do western talk?

KEN: (WESTERN DRAWL) Sure as shootin', pardner—right as rain—we're pals out here in the West where men are men, and women are glad of it, pardner.

ACE: OK, Ken, don't ham it up.

KEN: Smile when you say that, stranger.

MUSIC BRIDGE

ANDERSON: No, Jane, I don't think that's enough.

JANE: Well it's certainly different—he said he wanted something different. (DOOR OPENS AND CLOSES) And I think this is just what—oh, is that you, dear.

ACE: (OFF) Yes, Jane.

JANE: Well, dear, you missed it again. He just called again. Everytime you go out he calls.

ACE: Your customer?

JANE: Yes, you're never here when he calls.

ACE: Strange, isn't it?

ANDERSON: Yeah, I'm beginning to think it's very strange, if you know what I mean.

ACE: No, I don't know what you mean.

JANE: What do you mean, Sally?

ANDERSON: Jane, doesn't it strike you as peculiar that everytime that man calls your husband isn't here?

JANE: Sally, I just said that, please pay attention.

ACE: Yes, pay attention.

JANE: Dear, do you think this is novel enough—he said he wants something different—so I made this up. Happy Christmas, Merry New Year.

ACE: Happy Christmas?

JANE: Yeah, instead of visa firma. Instead of Merry Christmas, Happy—

ACE: Yes, I get it, Jane. But I don't think that's so novel. Here, I've got an idea—give me that pencil—now watch this—First you paint x-m-a-s—straight up and down— Now after the M you put "a-r-k-s."—Makes it Marks. After the S you write p-o-t—spot. Makes it spot. Now you've got X marks a Spot and under that you paint where I wish you a Merry Christmas and a Happy New Year.

JANE: Hey, dear, that's pretty good—look, Sally—did you see that?

ANDERSON: I'm still wondering why he's never here when those phone calls come in. Jane, I suspect foul play.

JANE: What are you talking about, Sally? You're always trying to complicate things, instead of trying to simplicate them.

ANDERSON: Well, it just strikes me as peculiar that he's never here when the phone rings.

ACE: Miss Anderson, are you implying that I made those phone calls?

JANE: *You*, dear! How could *you* make 'em—wouldn't I know your voice? Besides you're married. And where would you get a horse? You couldn't have called. Did you? (PHONE RINGS)

ACE: Jane, how could you doubt me.

ANDERSON: Jane, the telephone.

JANE: Oh the phone—now we'll see what's going on here or not. (PHONE UP) Hello.

KEN: (WESTERN) (FILTER) Hello there.

JANE: Uh—hold the phone, please. Hello, dear.

ACE: Hello, Jane, what's that for?

JANE: Sorry I doubted you, dear. Forgive me?

ACE: I'll think it over, Jane.

JANE: That's sweet. (WESTERN) Hello there, pardner.

KEN: Hello there, pardner.

JANE: Well we sure got a novel idea. The card is gonna say X-M-A-S—only we're gonna write in some extra words so it'll say X Marks a Spot where I wish you a Merry Christmas. You see?

KEN: Sounds great, pardner—mighty fine—I'll take a thousand of 'em.

JANE: A thousand—you want a thousand cards now?

ANDERSON: A thousand?

ACE: *Thousand*—what's he doing—

JANE: I thought you said you only wanted one—for your horse.

KEN: Just bought a thousand head of cattle, ma'am. Don't want no hard feelin's between my cattle and my horse.

JANE: But you know a thousand cards will cost a lot of money.

KEN: Money—what's money to me?

JANE: Just a minute, please—Sally, he wants a thousand cards —we'll have to buy more cards right away—more paint—

ACE: Wait a minute, Jane—this is getting out of hand—this little project is gonna run into money now—he doesn't want a thousand cards.

JANE: He did too. Here, *you* ask him if he didn't.

ACE: OK. Hello.

KEN: (WESTERN) Hello there, tenderfoot.

ACE: OK—take it easy—don't get carried away.

KEN: Hold on, stranger—what's *your* handle?

ACE: Enough is enough, if you know what I mean.

KEN: Enough—where I hail from down in Texas "enough" is for poor folks.

ACE: Very good—yes—but you better tell the ladies you don't really want a thousand cards.

JANE: Dear, don't say that—

KEN: Pardner, when I say a thousand, I mean a thousand.

ACE: Yes—yes—look, they're gonna run a printing bill—and paint—now let's don't overdo this thing—I don't want this to cost money.

JANE: Dear, gimme that phone.

KEN: Money—what's money to me, pardner—

ACE: All right, character actor—

KEN: I got oil wells—cotton gins—tobacco plantations—mint juleps—banjo on my knee—sun shines east, sun shines west, but I know where the sun shines best.

ACE: Look, Jolso—look, mister—I know you're rolling in money —but don't you think you better tell the ladies you wanta see one sample card first?

KEN: OK, pardner—I'll take a thousand sample cards.

ACE: One sample card, OK—

KEN: Down where I come from we don't take one of nothing.

ACE: Yes, sir, one sample, I'll tell them.

KEN: (FADING) I got oil wells—cotton gins—tobacco planta-tions—

MUSIC BRIDGE: DEEP IN THE HEART OF TEXAS

ACE: Well, that's what comes of giving an announcer too many lines to read. He nearly cost me a lot of money, but I convinced the Christmas card magnates to have only one card made. However, the next morning at the office there suddenly appeared on my desk some strange bills. I called in Miss Anderson. What are these bills for, Miss Anderson?

ANDERSON: Bills?

ACE: Yes, printer—paint company—radio station—you don't mean you and Jane have been charging all this stuff to me.

ANDERSON: Well, we're gonna pay it back from the money we make on the thousand cards.

ACE: Oh no—two hundred dollars' worth of bills I'm gonna be stuck for. (DOOR OPENS)

ANDERSON: But you're not stuck for it—we're gonna pay you back— (DOOR CLOSES)

JANE: Dear, guess what happened.

ANDERSON: Hello, Jane.

JANE: Sally—the printer just called me up.

ACE: Just a minute, Jane—you charged this two hundred dollars' worth of junk to me?

JANE: Well you don't have to worry about it, dear. You know that sample card I gave to Mr. O'Brien, the printer?

ACE: I'm not interested in—

JANE: He just called me up and he said he likes the idea so much he wants to buy it for five hundred dollars.

ACE: I'm not interested—five hundred dollars?

JANE: He just called me. Shall I take it?

ACE: Shall you take it? You'll take it and pay this two hundred dollars' worth of bills.

ANDERSON: Jane, we make three hundred dollars clear profit.

JANE: You see, Sally? That's the profit I was telling you

about. You see, dear, is that using the old chromium or isn't it?

ACE: Look, chromo, you're lucky I didn't get stuck for those bills. And after this please don't charge anything to— (DOOR OPENS)—this office.

KEN: (ENTERING) Hello, folks.

JANE: Ken, guess what happened. I sold the idea for five hundred dollars.

KEN: Yeh? Gee, that's great, Jane.

ANDERSON: Oh but, Jane, suppose that man calls for his Christmas cards.

ACE: Don't worry about that, he won't call. There isn't any customer.

JANE: How can you say that, dear?

ACE: How can I say that— (WESTERN) *Hello there.*

JANE: Oh there he is, Sally—you answer it, and tell him.

ACE: No, Jane, that was I. I was the one that called you.

JANE: *You?* You were there when he called?

KEN: (WESTERN) Hello there.

JANE: Oh there he is again. I'll answer this time.

KEN: Haha, no, Jane, I did that. I called last night. Pretty good, wasn't it? Haha.

ACE: Hahaha—that was a good one on you, wasn't it, Jane?

JANE: Oh yes? Well the laugh's on the other foot now— I made three hundred dollars, didn't we, Sally?

ANDERSON: And I know just what I'm gonna buy with my half, Jane.

JANE: Let's go shopping. We'll charge it, dear. And we'll pay you when we get the money from the printer.

ACE: OK—go ahead.

BOTH: (EXIT) (TALKING TOGETHER) I saw the cutest dress, Jane— I've gotta get some shoes—you come with me first—all right— (DOOR CLOSES)

ACE: Well that was a narrow escape. I almost got stuck for two hundred dollars—if they hadn't sold that thing to the printer—

KEN: Wait till they find out about that.

ACE: What?

KEN: (IRISH) Sure and I called Jane up and told her I was Mr. O'Brien, the printer, and I asked 'em would they be after taking five hundred dollars for their cards.

ACE: Oh no—

KEN: Son of the old sod—by Killarney's lakes and waters— with a banjo on my knee—

ACE: Isn't that awful.

MUSIC PLAYOFF

JANE'S MOTHER COMES TO VISIT

ACE: How about that one, Jane? What do you think?

JANE: You know what I've been thinking? How about a picture of you on the cover of the book by yourself?

ACE: You must be kidding. A picture of me on the cover is not going to sell any books.

JANE: Yes, I guess you're right.

ACE: Well now, just a minute. Let's not put me down so fast. Let's at least debate it.

JANE: No, I always say you can't judge a book by its lover.

ACE: OK, debate over. Next script. Now here's one I seem to remember rather fondly—with some reservations, the one where your mother came to visit.

JANE: Oh yes, I remember when you made those reservations.

MUSIC: MANHATTAN SERENADE
ACE: *Ladies and gentlemen, Easy Aces.*
MUSIC OUT

ACE: I learned years ago not to tell mother-in-law jokes.

In fact the first year we were married—I made an agree-ment with Jane that everytime I told a joke about her mother, I'd have to pay her a dollar. Barbara Hutton we called Jane that year . . . And besides what happened to me with Jane's mother this week was no joke. It started the other evening after dinner—I was reading the paper and Jane was writing a letter . . .

JANE: Oh my goodness, this doesn't look right. Dear, how do you spell write?

ACE: Write?

JANE: Yes, I'm answering my mother's letter and I'm having one of my bad spells.

ACE: Yes—which write do you mean—there's r-i-g-h-t and w-r-i-t-e. How are you using it? What's the word ahead of it?

JANE: Oh, the word ahead of it is last.

ACE: Oh, last rite! What's r-i-t-e . . . What happened? Why? Who was it? How old was he?

JANE: No, dear—all I'm saying is Dear Mother, I'm glad I found time to at last write you.

ACE: Oh! Last write—yes.

JANE: I'm answering this letter she sent me—would you like to hear it?

ACE: What's the other choice?

JANE: OK, I will. Oh, first let me tell you a very funny story I heard today, dear. There was a fellow that found a certain doctor charges ten dollars for the first visit, and five dollars for the second visit. So when he went to see him for the first time he said, "Hello, Doctor, here I am again."

Hahaha.

ACE: You heard that today?

JANE: Yes.

ACE: For the first time?

JANE: Yes, the first time it was ten dollars and the second time—

ACE: Don't *explain* it, Jane; I got it.

JANE: Well you're not laughing.

ACE: Oh excuse me, Jane. Hahahaha.

JANE: Hahaha. Well, now that we're all in a good mood, I'll read the letter. I'll get all the pages in order—ten— eleven—twelve—here we are.

ACE: Twelve pages? They wrote the Declaration of Independence on one page.

JANE: Well, they had those quill pens then.

ACE: Look, John Hancock, why don't you just condense what she says. How is your mother?

JANE: Oh, fair to meddling. She says, "Dear" uh— (oh she writes so badly)—yes—"Dear Jane: How are you? How is your husband? I hope you are both well and happy. I am as happy as can be expected since I've been living with your sister and her husband. Of course, I need a new upper plate, and I need a pair of new arch supports, and I could use a new hearing aid. The only thing I don't need is a pair of new glasses and your sister has to be married to an optician . . . But you know me, I never complain. Even when your sister's husband opened the kitchen door in my face, I kept a stiff upper lip . . . Your loving mother, Mother."

ACE: That's twelve pages?

JANE: P.S.

ACE: Oh, of course.

JANE: P.S.: "As I wrote you in my last letter, the doctor said the climate here is not good for me, and I should be near the seashore. So I am asking you if it's all right to come to visit you over the holidays."

ACE: Wait a minute—she lives in California. Why does she have to come to New York for the shore?

JANE: Dear—California's three thousand miles from the ocean.

ACE: Oh yes, I never thought of that.

JANE: When was I—oh yes—"If it isn't all right for me to come, I'll know it's not your fault, and you can tell him for me"—oh I'll skip this part.

ACE: No, no—I wanta hear that. And you can tell him for me what?

JANE: "You can tell him for me that I wouldn't ask to come if you hadn't written me that he said he needed me."

ACE: Who? When did I say that?

JANE: Last month—don't you remember when I said New York is so nice this time of year, I wish my mother was here, and you said, "That's all I need, is your mother."

ACE: Look, Jane—here's what I want you to write her: tell her she could stay in California and that I—

JANE: Wait a minute, I haven't finished reading the letter. Where was I—oh yes—that he needed me. "I wish you will let me know right away if I can come because I am desperate to get away from here, because this is a matter of life and—life and—I can't read this last word. Oh, she says in the next sentence—"please excuse the shaky handwriting because we have just left Kansas City and the train is going real fast."

ACE: Oh, *no*—isn't that awful?

MUSIC BRIDGE

ACE: The next morning at breakfast, a telegram came from Pittsburgh: "Arriving New York this afternoon at three o'clock your time. If it's too much trouble don't bother meeting me at the station, as I will probably not have one of my fainting spells right in the middle of the station, and if I should, some stranger will probably find me eventually, and besides I only have just the three bags and a small steamer trunk. Collect Mother—uh—love, Mother." (SOUND OF DISHES)

JANE: Well, I guess you're gonna be too busy to meet her, so I will.

ACE: Yes, I'm too busy. Have you broken the news to our maid yet that your mother's coming?

JANE: Mrs. Bell? Oh she'll love Mother. They have so much that's common.

ACE: Yes, I know, everybody loves your mother. But you better break it to Mrs. Bell gently.

JANE: All right. *Mrs. Bell.*

BELL: (OFF) What is it, Jane?

JANE: Can I see you a minute?

BELL: (OFF) I'm busy, Jane. I'm listening to the radio.

JANE: Oh. When you're finished, will you come in?

BELL: (OFF) OK, Jane.

ACE: Listening to the radio—is that all she does out there in the kitchen?

JANE: Well, she has her favorite radio programs. When she first came to work here I promised her she could listen to the radio.

BELL: (COMING IN) OK, Jane, what is it? I was just listening to *The Story of Laura Winthrop* which poses the problem can a mother-in-law find happiness having three children and visit each one of them four months a year, or will she have a better chance at happiness with four children and visit each one three months a year. How that mother-in-law has loused up Laura's life, they'll do it every time. What is it, Jane?

ACE: Well, Mrs. Bell, my mother-in-lous—mother-in-law—

JANE: Quiet, dear.

BELL: Yeh, quiet, dear—what is it, Jane?

JANE: Well, we're expecting a visitor.

BELL: Well, congratulations. Where's the cigar?

ACE: No, no, not that kind of a visitor. It's my mother-in-law.

BELL: Mother-in-law—not for me!

JANE: Wait a minute, Mrs. Bell—it's not his mother-in-law, it's my mother.

BELL: Look, Jane, when I took this job here you said there would be only two people. It's in my contract.

ACE: Contract. What kind of a contract?

BELL: I got it right here—I carry it around all the time—here's clause three—"party of the first part agrees that party of the second part will not have to wait on, serve, clean up after, cook for, make the beds of, and/or empty ash trays from more than two people at one time."

ACE: Who signed a thing like that? Not us.

BELL: I signed it.

ACE: You signed—

BELL: I'm the one who empties the ash trays, so why shouldn't I be the one who signs it.

ACE: But I didn't sign it.

BELL: Why should you? What do you do around here?

ACE: I'm the one that dirties the ash trays. Without me you'd have no job.

BELL: Ignorance of the law is no excuse.

ACE: Well, I gotta get to work. See you later, Jane.

JANE: But dear: what are we going to do about Mrs. Bell?

ACE: You girls work that out between you. (GOING) Goodbye, Jane—goodbye, Mrs. Bell. (DOOR OPENS . . . CLOSES)

JANE: Now, Mrs. Bell—

BELL: There's no use talking, Jane. I like to work for you, as long as there's two of you, but if you're gonna ring in a party of the third part, I'm going to strike.

JANE: Wait a minute, Mrs. Bell—where are you running to like a chicken with its hat off?

BELL: Jane which is it—me or your mother? One of us has to go.

JANE: Well, after all my mother is my own flesh and bones.

BELL: OK, Jane, I'm on strike. I'm going downstairs and picket.

JANE: Picket?

BELL: I'll walk up and down in front of the apartment and tell everybody you're unfair. And you can finish ironing those shirts in there yourself while I picket.

JANE: All right—if you're gonna strike, do it now; strike while the iron is hot.

MUSIC BRIDGE

ACE: Jane was having a problem at home with her maid, I was having a problem with my secretary at the office, Miss Anderson. She is Jane's cousin, and I'm stuck with her. Around two-thirty that afternoon, Miss Anderson buzzed me on the inter-office phone. She had just returned from her lunch hour and a half: (SOUND OF BUZZER . . . CLICK)

ACE: Yes?

ANDERSON: (FILTER) Mr. Ace, this is Miss Anderson.

ACE: Miss Anderson, I think I've explained to you before that this is an inter-office phone which connects your desk out there with mine in here—nobody else uses this phone. There are no party lines, no extensions and no co-axial cables. I *know* it's you, and if I answer you know it's me. You don't have to say, Mr. Ace, this is Miss Anderson speaking. Just say what you got to say and hang up quickly.

ANDERSON: Are you quite finished?

ACE: What do you want?

ANDERSON: Mr. Ace, if I weren't Jane's cousin, whom is your wife as well—

ACE: Whom is—

ANDERSON: I would really resent that you misconstrue everything I say and do. And unless I am sadly misconstrued, you *deliberately* misconstrue everything I say and do.

ACE: There seems to be a lot of unnecessary misconstruing going on around here. What is this misconstrue business?

ANDERSON: *Learn a word a day by using it every way*—It's in the newspaper every morning. Today's word is misconstrue. And if I choose to better my vocabulary are you gonna deliberately misconstrue that too?

ACE: Look, Miss Constru—look Miss Anderson—

ANDERSON: Everytime I buzz you on this inter-office phone we come to a complete misconstruction.

ACE: We do?

ANDERSON: I always make a supreme effort to construe you, the least you can do is construe me.

ACE: Isn't that awful?

ANDERSON: Answering an inter-office phone should in no way be mis-construable. Your misconstructive attitude is breaking down our whole construction.

ACE: Construction—what are you building up to? What did you call me for?

ANDERSON: Jane is on the phone.

ACE: I construe you—put her on. What I go through here with that—

JANE: (FILTER) Hello.

ACE: Hello, Jane.

JANE: This is Jane.

ACE: I know who you are—you've been announced—I said, Hello Jane—now what is it?

JANE: Mrs. Bell is striking.

ACE: Oh, I wouldn't say striking. "Attractive," maybe.

JANE: No, I mean she's striking—she says I'm unfair.

ACE: Oh, Jane, I think you're the fairest in the land.

JANE: You do, dear? Oh you do not.

ACE: Yes, I do.

JANE: You do? Oh you do not.

ACE: Yes, I do.

JANE: You do? Oh you do not.

ACE: OK, I don't.

JANE: I knew it wouldn't last.

ACE: Jane—what is it—what's on your mind?

JANE: I told you—Mrs. Bell went on a strike—she's picketing— she's walking to and from in front of the apartment. She's got a big sign that says *Mrs. Ace is unfair.* Don't you think that's terrible?

ACE: Yes, I do.

JANE: You do? Oh you do not.

ACE: Don't start that again.

JANE: What shall I do about Mrs. Bell? I have to prepare dinner—she quit work. And I can't find the roasting pan. I looked high and dry, I can't find hide or seek of it. It's behind me where she put it.

ACE: Have you looked in the refrigerator?

JANE: Refrigerator—oh stop being silly. I'll have to go downstairs and ask Mrs. Bell. But dear, you'll have to go meet my mother at the station.

ACE: Me?

JANE: She gets in at three o'clock, now you be there.

ACE: OK, Jane—I've got a full calendar of appointments and everything, but I have to drop everything and go meet your mother. This is certainly going to misconstrue up my whole day.

JANE: Do what?

ACE: Learn a word a day—use it every way. Goodbye, Jane.

MUSIC BRIDGE

ACE: When I got to the station I found the train would be two hours late. It seemed they had to back up at Altoona to pick up a car which had been uncoupled by a little old lady who had complained the train was going too fast. And while I was waiting for her, Jane was down on the street in front of our apartment trying to find out where the roasting pan was. (SOUND OF STREET NOISES)

BELL: *Mrs. Ace is unfair to maids . . . Mrs. Ace is unfair to maids.*

JANE: Mrs. Bell, for the last time, will you tell me where the roasting pan is?

BELL: In the refrigerator. *Mrs. Ace is unfair to maids.*

JANE: Please, Mrs. Bell—people will hear you.

BELL: I want 'em to hear me. *Mrs. Ace is unfair to maids.*

JANE: Do you have to holler it like that? That sign you're carrying says the same thing.

BELL: I have to holler it for people who can't read. *Mrs. Ace is unfair to maids.*

JANE: Well you're unfair to me. You hid that roasting pan, and the least you can do is go in and find it so I can get dinner.

BELL: I can't go in now, Jane. I'm busy picketing. I gotta carry this sign.

JANE: Oh, all right, give me the sign. I'll carry it.

BELL: Well—OK, Jane. But hold it up high.

JANE: Like this?

BELL: That's it, Jane—way up high so everybody can see it. And you've gotta talk it up.

JANE: What?

BELL: Keep saying *Mrs. Ace is unfair to maids.*

JANE: Oh all right—Mrs. Ace is unfair to maids—Mrs. Ace is unfair to maids.

BELL: Louder.

JANE: Want me to strain my yokel chords? *Mrs. Ace is unfair to maids.* Is that better?

BELL: That's the ticket, Jane—keep walking and talking.

JANE: *Mrs. Ace is unfair to maids. Mrs. Ace is unfair to maids.* Well, why don't you go up and find the roasting pan?

BELL: I'm sorry, Jane, I can't. I can't cross a picket line.

KEN: Hey, what's going on, Jane?

JANE: Oh hello, Ken. It's Ken Roberts, Mrs. Bell.

KEN: Hello, Mrs. Bell.

BELL: Hi, Ken.

KEN: What's the trouble here—what does that mean you're unfair to maids?

BELL: It's in my contract. I only have to serve two people— and now she rings a mother-in-law on me.

JANE: She's my mother—not mother-in-law—she's coming to visit me. And Mrs. Bell is on strike.

KEN: Oh now, wait a minute—you shouldn't strike about a thing like that. How about a little mediation?

BELL: Never touch a thing in the middle of the day.

KEN: No, Mrs. Bell, I mean you can reach some agreement. Jane, can't you make some concession?

JANE: I can't make anything. I can't find the roasting pan.

KEN: You don't understand, Jane—I mean you can bargain

collectively. Like this. Mrs. Bell, suppose Mrs. Ace gave you something extra for the extra person, would that be all right?

BELL: Something extra—like what?

KEN: Well, let me see—you don't live with the Aces now, do you, Mrs. Bell?

BELL: No, I have a room—I pay rent.

KEN: Well, if they gave you a room to live in with them— that would save you rent—would that be OK, Mrs. Bell?

BELL: Oh sure, Ken.

KEN: Well, how about it, Jane?

JANE: What? What happened? I wasn't listening. I just noticed on this sign she's got "Mrs. Ace" in smaller letters than "maids." That's unfair.

KEN: Jane, Mrs. Bell says if you'll give her a room with you, she'll come back to work.

JANE: We only have one guest room. My mother was gonna sleep in there.

BELL: *Mrs. Ace is unfair to—*

JANE: Oh, wait a minute; I didn't say no. Now let me see if you took that guest room, my mother could sleep with me—and then he could have the couch in the living room—it *is* a little small—yes, I guess it would be all right. OK, Mrs. Bell.

BELL: OK, Jane. That's a deal. Shake on it.

JANE: What?

BELL: Shake hands on it.

JANE: Oh. How do you do, Mrs. Bell.

MUSIC BRIDGE

ACE: Well, I finally got 'em all home, the old lady and the three other bags—I mean the three bags and the steamer trunk. We got home rather late. We had a little trouble in the taxi. She wanted to uncouple the meter, because we were going too fast. Then she asked me if we got her telegram, and I said no, I always go down to Penn Station and watch the trains come in. And all the way home she kept saying what a lucky coincidence it was. And I kept telling myself she'll only be here till after the holidays. When we got home Jane was so happy to see her.

JANE: Oh, Mother, I'm so happy to see you.

MOTHER: Happy. If it makes you happy to be happy, you be happy.

JANE: How was the train trip, Mother?

MOTHER: I got train sick. I should have taken a plane.

JANE: Well, why didn't you?

MOTHER: I get plane sick.

ACE: Well, why didn't you stay ho—

MOTHER: What did you say?

ACE: I said did you have nice accommodations on the train?

MOTHER: Oh yes, very nice. My daughter who I was staying with in California's husband got me a very nice compartment.

JANE: Oh that's nice, Mother.

MOTHER: They must have told the conductor to take good care of me. Because every time the train came to a station he locked me in my compartment.

ACE: Hm. How's everything in California?

JANE: Ethel writes me they're very happy out there.

MOTHER: Happy. Everybody's happy.

JANE: Do you ever see any movies stars, Mother?

MOTHER: Movies stars. Greer Garson lives one block from us. I wouldn't walk across the street to see her. Irene Dunne lives around the corner—I wouldn't walk across the street to see her. Clark Gable lives eight miles from us. Janie, I have to get some new arch supports.

JANE: All right, Mother—but how about Gregory Peck—ever see him?

MOTHER: Yes, I see him.

JANE: You did? How about Jimmy Stewart?

MOTHER: Yes, I see him too.

JANE: How about Ava Gardner?

MOTHER: I see him too.

ACE: Ava Gardner happens to be a woman.

MOTHER: If it makes him happy to be a woman, let him be happy.

JANE: Mother don't you wanta lie down before dinner—take a little sneeze?

MOTHER: Oh you don't have to bother about me, Janie—

I won't be a bother—I've never been a bother—you can ask your sister—I never bothered her—she never bothered about me—what can you expect from children? So if it's gonna be any bother, don't bother, because I don't wanta be a bother.

ACE: Is that the word for today?

JANE: Oh, Mother, you misconstrued me—

ACE: That's the word.

JANE: It won't be a bother. I won't have to bother. We got a maid that bothers. Mrs. Bell. I'll call her. *Mrs. Bell.*

BELL: (OFF) What do you want, Jane?

JANE: Can you come in a minute and meet my mother?

BELL: (OFF) Just a minute, Jane.

MOTHER: You've got a maid, now, Janie?

JANE: Yes, Mrs. Bell.

MOTHER: Are maids expensive, I suppose?

JANE: Well—

MOTHER: They don't work for nothing.

JANE: Oh no.

MOTHER: Do you pay her out of your allowance?

JANE: Yes, I pay her out of my allowance.

MOTHER: Then it must be a pretty *big* allowance, is it, Janie?

JANE: Yes, I think it—

MOTHER: Then if he gives you a big allowance, I suppose he's doing pretty well.

JANE: Oh yes, pretty well.

MOTHER: Well, when you pay your maid, the money you have left, what percentage is it of your allowance?

JANE: Percentage?

MOTHER: I mean like if you paid her thirty dollars a week, for instance, do you have thirty dollars a week left over?

JANE: Well, something like that.

MOTHER: Something like that—then that would be sixty—well what percentage would you say sixty is of his salary every week?

JANE: Percentage?

MOTHER: Well, let me put it this way—How much does—

ACE: A hundred and fifty dollars a week . . .

MOTHER: Before or after taxes?

ACE: Isn't that awful.

BELL: (COMING IN) Yeh, Jane, here I am.

JANE: Oh come in, Mrs. Bell—this is my mother, Mrs. Sherwood, Mrs. Bell.

MOTHER: I'm pleased to meet you Mrs. Bell.

BELL: Hello, Mom. I'm happy to meet you.

MOTHER: Happy. Everybody's happy. With your money I'd be happy too.

BELL: What?

JANE: Mrs. Bell, Mother has to have something special for dinner.

BELL: Special? Like what?

MOTHER: I don't want to be any bother—if it's going to be a bother, don't bother. Just a boiled egg, that's all.

BELL: A boiled egg? That's all you want for dinner?

MOTHER: That's all—on top of the spinach.

BELL: Spinach? What spinach?

MOTHER: The spinach that goes with the boiled tongue.

BELL: Boiled tongue? We haven't any boiled tongue.

JANE: We're having a roast for dinner, Mother.

MOTHER: Well, I'll take roast. I don't want to be a bother. There are only a few things I'm allowed to eat—tongue, roast chicken, hamburger steak, veal chops, duck, and once in a while a little corned beef and cabbage.

ACE: What can't you eat?

MOTHER: Peanut brittle. But if it makes you happy to have peanut brittle, be happy. I don't wanta be a bother.

JANE: Come on, Mother, I'll show you to your room and you can lie down a while.

MOTHER: (GOING) All right, Janie. Maybe I better rest a while.

JANE: (OFF) We'll have dinner late, Mother, so you can rest. We'll eat any time you want to.

MOTHER: (GOING) Oh it doesn't matter to me, Janie—I'm never hungry—what time is it now? (DOOR OPENS)

JANE: Five-fifteen.

MOTHER: All right—so wake me up at five-thirty. But if it's

gonna be a bother, don't bother. I don't want to be a bother. (DOOR CLOSES)

ACE: You see, Mrs. Bell—she doesn't want to be a bother. And it's only till after the holidays.

BELL: Oh, don't worry about me, I'll be able to handle Laughing Girl.

ACE: I'm happy to hear you say that, Mrs. Bell.

BELL: If it makes you happy to be happy—

ACE: Oh no—not you too.

MUSIC BRIDGE

ACE: Well I wanta tell you something—it did my heart good to see that sweet little old lady pack away that dinner. Because if she packs it away like that three times a day she'll never *last* till after the holidays. I still didn't know about this arrangement Jane had made for Mrs. Bell to live with us. I should have suspected something when we were sitting around the living room after dinner—and Mrs. Bell had finished the dishes—and she walked in, sat next to me on the love seat, put her feet on the coffee table, took out a cigarette, and turned to me and said:

BELL: How's about a match, dear?

ACE: What?

BELL: A match.

ACE: Oh—yes—here—

JANE: Oh, I didn't tell you, did I, dear?

ACE: Tell me what?

JANE: Mrs. Bell is gonna live with us while mother's here.

ACE: Gonna live with us?

JANE: She was on strike, and Ken Roberts made up the meditation.

ACE: Meditation—

JANE: Yes—you know—when two people disagree, they have to meditate. So Mrs. Bell is gonna live with us.

ACE: Just a minute—let me meditate on that.

MOTHER: Thirty dollars a week and she lives here besides.

ACE: But Jane, we only have one guest room.

JANE: A very good question, dear. And the answer is the living-room couch.

ACE: What about the living-room couch?

JANE: Well, somebody has to sleep on the couch . . . (PAUSE)

MOTHER: I think I'll go to my room and lie down.

ACE: Room—

BELL: Just a minute, Mom, we're still meditatin'.

ACE: We certainly are. Who sleeps on the couch, that's what I want to know.

JANE: Now just a minute, dear, don't jump at convulsions. Let's figure it out—we'll put our heads together.

ACE: That's fine—that puts you and me in our bedroom.

JANE: Yes. Now Mother takes the guest room, and Mrs. Bell sleeps on the couch.

BELL: Not me, Jane.

MOTHER: With the money you make, you can get a penthouse at the Waldorf.

JANE: Well, now wait a minute—we'll figure out another way. Dear, you and Mrs. Bell will—no that won't do. Dear, if you and Mother—no, that won't do. Well, Mother and Mrs. Bell.

MOTHER AND BELL: *Oh no.*

JANE: No, that won't do. Don't worry, dear, I'll figure it out. Mrs. Bell doesn't wanta sleep on the couch, and mother *can't* sleep on the couch—and I go without saying—so that leaves—

ACE: No!

JANE: But, dear, it's only till after the holidays.

BELL: Yeh, dear, only till after the holidays.

ACE: Only till after the holidays—isn't this awful—well, all right, I don't wanta be a bother—if I'm gonna be a bother, don't bother bothering. I'll sleep on the couch.

JANE: You see, dear, it was so simple.

ACE: Yes, I am. Mother, you *are* going back after the holidays aren't you, Mother?

MOTHER: Yes, I got my return ticket already.

ACE: You wouldn't mind showing it to me?

MOTHER: If it'll make you happy to see it, here, be happy. There's the ticket. You can see the return date is punched on it.

ACE: Where?

MOTHER: Right there—July fifth.

ACE: July fifth. Jane, you said only till after the holidays.

JANE: Yes. Christmas, New Year's, Valentine's Day, Washington's Birthday, Lincoln's Birthday, April Fool's Day, Mother's Day, Father's Day, Decoration Day—

ACE: (FADING) Yes, till Doomsday. Isn't that awful?

MUSIC PLAYOFF

JANE GOES TO A PSYCHIATRIST

JANE: I don't think that was nice, making jokes about my
mother.

ACE: Well you know I didn't mean it, Jane. Much. Now here's
a program we did about your going to see a psychiatrist.

JANE: And you know that's not true either. I think people
who go to a psychiatrist ought to have their heads ex-
amined.

ACE: Hey, that's very clever.

JANE: You do? Oh, it was nothing really.

ACE: Exactly.

MUSIC: MANHATTAN SERENADE
ACE: *Ladies and gentlemen, Easy Aces*
MUSIC OUT

ACE: Well, I tried to stop her, but Jane insisted she had to go
to a psychiatrist. After a week of visits, and with a little
rest and care, I'm happy to announce that the psychiatrist will be out in a few months. Psychoanalysis, you know,
was developed by Freud, late in the nineteenth century.

But it never got popular till it was taken over by Fox in the Twentieth Century . . . Jane's interest in the couch started the other day—when she met my boss's wife, Mrs. Norris, on the street, and they had a chat about psychoanalysis. Went something like this:

MARGARET: Well, Mrs. Ace, good morning.

JANE: Oh hello, Mrs. Norris, long face no see.

MARGARET: Yes. Where are you going, my dear?

JANE: Just fine.

MARGARET: Well, how've you been?

JANE: Oh just up to the corner to match this material for a dress.

MARGARET: That's good.

JANE: I hardly recognized you, Mrs. Norris—it's that sweater you're wearing, I guess.

MARGARET: Oh my sweater. Do you like it?

JANE: Oh, you look stunned.

MARGARET: My dear, I've never worn a sweater before I started going to my psychoanalyst—he told me my subconscious mind kept me from wearing it—and he made me get rid of my inhibitions. He did a good job on me, I can tell you that.

JANE: Oh yes, he certainly fitted it well.

MARGARET: His name is Dr. Montel.

JANE: Dr. who?

MARGARET: Montel—M-o-n-t-e-l. He adjusts all your mental conflicts. It's done wonders for me, my dear. Every night I offer up thanks for Freud.

JANE: For who?

MARGARET: Freud. F-r-e-u-d. He's the man who founded psychoanalysis. Oh, what Dr. Montel could do for *you*, my dear. He'll tell you everything that's on your mind.

JANE: Well, all I have on my mind now is this material I wanta get matched for a dress—

MARGARET: Oh no, I mean on your subconscious mind. Things you don't even know are there yourself. For instance: look at me and Jonathan. He's as devoted a husband as you'll find anywhere. And still, in spite of all his devotion, it has left me—shall I say apathetic?

JANE: All right.

MARGARET: Last week, for instance, he said to me, "Margaret," he said, "you're certainly looking well." It was then I realized I had to see a psychoanalyst. Because my subconscious mind said to me, "Yes, he thinks you look well now, but how *long* will he think you look well?" That's when I went to see Dr. Montel. And what he's done for me. He told me what makes me tick. My dear, you simply must go to him at once.

JANE: First I have to get this material matched for a dress . . .

MARGARET: Oh, I don't mean this minute. You'll have to make an appointment. He's so busy, and so handsome. You can see what he's done for my mental conflicts.

JANE: Yes, you're so cheerful and so ravenous looking in that sweater—maybe I will go.

MARGARET: Tell him I sent you. Do you remember the name?

JANE: Oh sure—Mrs. Norris.

MARGARET: No, I mean the doctor's name. Dr. Montel.

JANE: Oh yes, F-r-e-u-d.

MUSIC BRIDGE

ACE: All through dinner that evening I noticed there was something on Jane's—if you'll pardon the four letter word—mind. And after dinner she sat there staring into space—so I sat there staring into space. We stared into each other's space. And finally she said:

JANE: Dear, how do I look to you?

ACE: Vapid.

JANE: Yes, but how *long* will I look that way?

ACE: Well, according to insurance statistics, your life expectancy is about—

JANE: No, you're getting off the subject. Do I look good to you—that's what I want to know. Now come on, I want your candied opinion.

ACE: My candied opinion is that you look very sweet—wonderful.

JANE: Oh my. I've got it too.

ACE: I beg your pardon—what have you got?

JANE: Mental Conflicts. M-e-n-t-a-l—

ACE: Isn't that awful . . . What are you talking about?

JANE: I'm going to a psychoanalyst first thing in the morning.

ACE: To a psychoanalyst! Jane, you amaze me.

JANE: Not now, dear. Let me tell you why I decided to go to him. This morning I ran into Mrs. Norris.

ACE: Hard, I trust.

JANE: And she told me she's been going to him—and you should see what he's done for her. She's wearing a sweater.

ACE: She went to a psychiatrist so she could wear a—

JANE: She got rid of all her exhibitions.

ACE: Not in a sweater she didn't.

JANE: And just now when you said to me how wonderful I look, it left me, shall I say, apathetic?

ACE: Apathetic.

JANE: A-p-a-t—

ACE: *Will you stop spelling at me?* I know apathetic. And you're not going to a psychoanalyst.

JANE: He doesn't give you a medicine, you know—

ACE: I know—I know.

JANE: I tell him what's on my *mind*, and *he* tells me what's on *my* mind.

ACE: Jane, he wouldn't have a target.

JANE: Don't you understand, dear, when you told me just now I look wonderful, and I felt shall I say apathetic, that means something.

ACE: It means you look wonderful.

JANE: Yes, but how *long* will you think I look wonderful?

ACE: How long!

JANE: See, even you're beginning to wonder.

ACE: No I'm not! Jane, we have no money to throw away on foolishness like that. They're expensive.

JANE: Yes but look what he does for you. He told Mrs. Norris all about herself—told her what makes her thick.

ACE: And she is. Jane if you go to this guy you'll wind up in a straitjacket.

JANE: Well, if he fits it for me, as well as he did her sweater—

ACE: He will—he will.

MUSIC BRIDGE

ACE: So the next morning Jane got up bright and early and went to see the psychoanalyst. *Correction*—The next morning Jane got up early and went to see the psychoanalyst. The doctor was ready for her with pencil and couch:

MONTEL: And you say Mrs. Norris sent you to see me?

JANE: Yes, she did, Dr. Montel.

MONTEL: Mrs. Norris . . . Oh yes—she had a deep-seated neurosis. Why *will* people permit their neurosis to become so deep seated? If they would only come to me earlier.

JANE: Well, you said eleven-thirty, Dr. Montel.

MONTEL: Mrs. Ace, for your first visit I'll take your case history. Are you comfortable on that couch?

JANE: Oh this is fine, thank you. I like your office—everything Mrs. Norris told me about you is certainly true, Dr. Montel. She said you were handsome.

MONTEL: Really—well now I—

JANE: And may I return the compliment and say *I* think you're handsome too.

MONTEL: Well—now—so much for the doctor. Let's get to the patient. Tell me about yourself, Mrs. Ace.

JANE: Well, I wouldn't say I'm handsome exactly. But my husband thinks I—

MONTEL: Let's not discuss your husband for our first visit—let's stick to you. Tell me, how do you feel—generally, I mean.

JANE: Well, physically—if you'll pardon the expression—I feel fine. But it's the mental conflicts that get me.

MONTEL: What mental conflicts?

JANE: Like when my husband said last night I look wonderful; my unconscious said, "How long will I look that way?"

MONTEL: Ah ha.

JANE: Ah ha.

MONTEL: Something on the order of Mrs. Norris's anxiety neurosis. Well, I see I'll have to prescribe for you the same as I did for her.

JANE: Yes, I guess so. Except that I wear a much smaller size than she does.

MONTEL: What?

JANE: What what?

MONTEL: Uh—Mrs. Ace, tell me, how long have you had these thoughts when someone compliments you on your appearance.

JANE: Since I saw Mrs. Norris yesterday.

MONTEL: Oh, then I'm sure yours is a mild case and I can cure you in this one visit.

JANE: But if I'm always going to say 'How long' to myself—

MONTEL: You won't always say that. I'm sure you won't. Mrs. Ace, I think you're a very charming woman.

JANE: Well, thank you, Dr. Montel. I guess it's this new blouse I'm wearing—

MONTEL: There, you see—you accepted my flattery without a single thought to the contrary passing through your mind.

JANE: Yes, sir, I did.

MONTEL: You're cured, Mrs. Ace. It was a simple case. You don't need a psychoanalyst. But I'm glad you got here when you did. Most people wait till it's too late.

JANE: Well, I'm sure glad I got here at the psychopathic moment.

MONTEL: Yes. And there are too many more important cases in these troubled ti—these troubled—what did you say? When? You got here at what moment?

JANE: The psychopathic moment.

MONTEL: Psychopathic—

JANE: Yes. Well, goodbye, Doctor—how much do I owe—

MONTEL: No—no—just a moment—lie back please.

JANE: What happened?

MONTEL: Say that again. You got here when? Say it.

JANE: Dr. Montel, you're scaring me—you're getting my bearings bawled up.

MONTEL: Getting your what?

JANE: Doctor, let me up—you're making a mountain out of Mohammed.

MONTEL: A mountain out of Mohammed.

JANE: Is something wrong?

MONTEL: Lie back, Mrs. Ace—you're a most interesting case.

JANE: I am, huh? I had a tuition there was gonna be trouble in the offering.

MONTEL: Tuition—hm—offering—yes, most interesting. Mrs. Ace, there is some force at work on your mind, which telegraphs twisted and hastily visualized words to your tongue—what *is* that force? That's what I want to find out. In the interest of research—would you come to me for an hour every day and tell me the story of your life from as far back as you can remember? Just one hour every day, will you come?

JANE: Sure, if you think I have to.

MONTEL: Yes—yes. Very interesting case. We'll have our first hour now—lie back, Mrs. Ace, and tell me the story of your life, from as far back as you can remember.

JANE: Well, let me see—I'll start with my five years in high school.

MONTEL: *Four* years, Mrs. Ace.

JANE: Not me, Doctor.

MUSIC BRIDGE

ACE: That night I refused to listen to anything Jane had to say about her visit to the psychoanalyst. But Jane found an interested audience in her mother, who is now living on us—with us. I oughta tell you about Jane's poor mother—she's in the last stages of a big appetite. She's been to every doctor in New York City, including one veterinarian in Flushing. That was the day she said she was sick as a dog. And she takes dozens of different medicines. There's one medicine she takes every hour on the hour. It's Cuttee—Sark—some Indian remedy, something like that. So when Jane mentioned having gone to a doctor, her mother looked up quickly and said:

MOTHER: So the doctor said you've got psychoanalysis? It sounds exciting, Janie. Did he give you a prescription?

JANE: No, Mother, he's not like the doctors that give you medicine, and take X-rays, and put you in an oxydol tent.

MOTHER: What kind of a doctor is that?

JANE: He's a psychoanalyst. He cures the mental conflicts, and he makes you happy.

MOTHER: Well if it makes you happy to be happy, be happy. Personally any doctor who won't give you medicine is a fraud.

JANE: That's right, F-r-e-u-d. He tells me what's on my mind. He can see right into my brain. Dear, now you stop that.

ACE: I didn't say anything.

JANE: Well I don't like your altitude about this whole thing. Stay out of this.

ACE: I don't like your spending money on psychoanalysis.

MOTHER: Money—after all what is money for, if not to spend

on doctors. I always say it's better to be well for one day, than sick for two weeks.

JANE: I'm not sick, Mother. Look, here's the whole thing in a nut house . . .

MOTHER: Just tell me about the doctor, Janie. He sounds very interesting.

JANE: A good question, Mother, and the answer is he certainly is. And the handsomest man you ever saw—with office to match. Tall—dark brown hair.

ACE: I've always wanted a tall office with dark brown hair.

JANE: And when he smiles—oh boy.

ACE: No teeth?

JANE: Dear, what did I tell you?

ACE: You said stay out of it.

JANE: Well do it. Where was I—

MOTHER: The doctor, Janie. Does he have a regular doctor's office?

JANE: Oh sure, like every doctor's office. Young nurse, old magazines. And you have to lie back on this couch he has there and talk to him. There's a table on either side of the couch—on one table cigars—on the other cigarettes. And he says to me, lie down and relapse, so I did. And he said, I want you to tell me the story of your life from as far back as you can remember. You can smoke if you want to, he said. So I took a cigar and started to talk.

ACE: Took a cigar?

JANE: It's in my bag, I'll give it to you later.

ACE: Oh. For me.

JANE: You see I'm always thinking of you, and you sit there making sarcastic remarks.

MOTHER: So what did you talk to him about? Did you tell him where it hurts you?

JANE: Oh no, Mother, I told him all about what I did when I was in high school. It wasn't very interesting. He yawned a couple of times, but I can take a hint. So tomorrow when I go, I'm gonna make up a story to tell him.

ACE: Make up a story?

JANE: Well, I'm certainly not gonna sit there boring him for a full hour every day. So tomorrow, I'm going to make up a story out of whole wheat. He said it's a good thing I went to him as early as I did. Most people wait till it's too late. Like Mrs. Norris for instance—do you want me to become deep-seated like Mrs. Norris?

ACE: No, Jane, that I don't.

MUSIC BRIDGE

ACE: Well, this is Friday, the day Jane hurried down to the psychoanalyst's office to continue telling him the story of her life—only she noticed he yawned through most of the story she told him yesterday, so today she has made up a lot of exciting things that didn't happen to hold his interest. This is the day which will set back psychoanalysis twenty-five years, one which became known in medical circles as Black Freudday.

MONTEL: That's it, Mrs. Ace . . . just lie back and relax and we'll take up where we left off yesterday. I hope we can do as well today as we did during our first hour.

JANE: Oh, this is gonna be a thriller diller, Doctor.

MONTEL: Yes. Let's take from after your high school graduation.

JANE: Yes. Well, sir, Doctor—oh you're gonna like this—it was the summer I graduated. The heat was on. And we were driving home from a party. Sally Anderson and I —and two fellows. The fellow she was with later left town, the fellow I was with, later became Mr. Ace—my husband . . . You see, Sally and I always double dated . . . we've been insufferable friends for years.

MONTEL: Insufferable—ah ha!

JANE: Oh yes, always together like a couple of simonized twins.

MONTEL: Simonized—yes, go on.

JANE: Yes, sir. Well, we were in the car and one of the boys was driving. The one in front. I was in front with him. Sally was in back with other one. We were singing and laughing—"Shine on Harvest Moon"—you know how school kids are—fool face and fancy free.

MONTEL: Fool face—ah ha.

JANE: Yes, you know—just out for a good time—not wild or anything like that . . . Or would you *prefer* wild?

MONTEL: What's that?

JANE: No, I guess you wouldn't. Well, we were driving along, when alongside our car came another car—and in that car was another boy I used to go with and he was jealous

that I was out with Mr. Ace who later became my husband. So I leaned over to Sally in the front seat and I
said, Isn't that Roy? And she said—

MONTEL: Just a moment, Mrs. Ace—you said before *you* were
in the front seat?

JANE: Oh did I? Well, Sally leaned over to *me* in the front
seat, and *I* said, Isn't that Roy? Is that better?

MONTEL: Yes, I believe it is.

JANE: And Sally said, Yes, I believe it is. Well, Roy was so
mad I was out with Mr. Ace who later became my husband that he wasn't watching where he was driving and he
almost bumped into us—he looked kinda wild—almost
besmerk, you might say.

MONTEL: Ah ha.

JANE: Ah ha. So Mr. Ace, the one who later became my
husband, started to drive faster to get away from him.
And pretty soon we were both going so fast—well, I'll
tell you how fast we were going—we were twelve miles
from town—and would you believe we made it in eight
miles?

MONTEL: You—made—it—in eight—miles—

JANE: Eight miles if I'm a day. And then to clap the climax—
we suddenly heard the whistle of a train coming around
the hill. Oh I forgot to tell you there was a hill—around
the bend—and we had to cross the tracks—but there we
were, going like bats out of a bellfry . . .

MONTEL: Bellfry—yes.

JANE: And we were going so fast we couldn't stop—and the
train was going even faster—we could hear the train

whistle—whoo whoo—and we were going Oh Oh—we all knew that if something didn't happen this was the end ... Well goodbye, Doctor, I'll see you tomorrow.

MONTEL: Wait a minute—what *happened?*

JANE: My hour is up, Doctor—to be continued tomorrow.

MUSIC BRIDGE

ACE: Well the story Jane made up out of whole wheat turned out to be a serial. While Dr. Montel was hurrying over to see *his* psychoanalyst, Jane rushed home to tell her mother and me what had happened on her second day's visit to the good doctor's office.

JANE: Well, sir, dear, he didn't yawn today. I told him a story about being in a car with you, who later became Mr. Ace, husband, and a train was coming around the hill and it looked like it was gonna hit the car—and then I stopped. Well you could have knocked him over with a fender.

ACE: You mean to say you told him the story up to that point and walked out?

JANE: Well, I haven't figured up a finish yet.

ACE: Isn't that awful.

MOTHER: But Janie, I don't understand—didn't the doctor even examine for bruises you might have gotten in the accident with the train?

JANE: Oh no, Mother—you don't understand—he isn't that kind of a doctor. He's a doctor for mental conflicts.

MOTHER: Mental conflicts? I never had those, Janie—is it anything like dizzy spells?

JANE: Oh no—mental conflicts. It's for people who worry.

MOTHER: Worry. Who doesn't worry? Except my sister, your Aunt Wilma. She used to worry all the time. And then one day she decided to stop worrying, and overnight her hair turned brown.

JANE: Mother, maybe you better come with me to see Dr. Montel.

ACE: I lost track here. Jane, you're not going back there tomorrow.

JANE: Oh I have to go back—I have to figure out a finish for that story and tell it to him. Wait a minute—tomorrow I can't go. I took some material to the dressmaker the other day—I have to go for a fitting. Dear.

ACE: What.

JANE: You'll go in my place.

ACE: You want me to go be psychoanalyzed in your place?

JANE: Unless you wanta go in my place to the dressmaker for a fitting.

ACE: Yes, I will go, Jane I want to visit that doctor. Maybe I can help him.

MUSIC BRIDGE

ACE: The next morning I went to see Dr. Montel. His office was just as Jane had described it, tall, dark brown, and I was greeted by a short nurse with a leather seat, at a desk.

NURSE: Good morning. May I help you?

ACE: I want to see Dr. Montel.

NURSE: Do you have an appointment?

ACE: Yes—eleven o'clock.

NURSE: What's the name?

ACE: Mrs. Ace.

NURSE: Oh yes—I have it in my book right here. (PAUSE) *Mrs.* Ace?

ACE: Yes, Jane Ace.

NURSE: Oh, to be sure. Well—well, the doctor will see you in a minute. Won't you have a chair, MRS. Ace?

ACE: No, no, you don't understand—you see . . . oh well— yes, thank you. I'll sit right here.

NURSE: No no, not here. Over there against the wall. That's it, Mrs. Ace—just relax—the doctor will be with you in a moment. Don't get excited—don't be nervous. Everything's going to be all right.

ACE: I'm not excited—I'm not nervous.

NURSE: That's right—just relax. The doctor will buzz when he's ready for you.

ACE: Thank you.

NURSE: Haha yes.

ACE: Haha yes. (SILENCE)

NURSE: Well, you're looking well today, Mrs. Ace.

ACE: It's just this make-up.

NURSE: Pancake?

ACE: Well, no, thank you, I just had breakfast.

NURSE: Uh . . . the doctor will see you in just a moment, Mrs. Ace. Would you like to look at this magazine?

ACE: Well yes, I don't mind—

NURSE: No, no, don't get up—I'll slide it over to you across the floor.

ACE: Oh thank you. Oh, the *Ladies' Home Journal*, yes.

NURSE: Yes. There are lovely new dress designs in this month's issue.

ACE: That reminds me—I wonder how I'm making out with that dress I'm having fitted over at the dressmaker's.

NURSE: You're having a fitting at the dressmaker's later on, Mrs. Ace?

ACE: No, I'm over there being fitted now.

NURSE: The doctor will see you in just a moment, Mrs. Ace.

ACE: Thank you. Yes, I have to go to the dressmaker for everything. I just simply can't find my size in ready mades. Even hose, I have to have 'em made special.

NURSE: Me too, Mrs. Ace. And the nylons they sell you these days. This morning I put on a brand-new pair of nylons and no sooner did I get here when I got a run in 'em. All the way up to here.

ACE: Really? Up to where?

NURSE: Look, Mrs. Ace—all the way up to—(BUZZER)—oh the doctor will see you right now, Mrs. Ace.

ACE: Now he sees me. This is pyschoanalysis?

NURSE: Go right in.

ACE: Thank you. It's been nice almost seeing you.

NURSE: Remember me to Mr. Ace.

MONTEL: (OFF) Come, come in, Mrs. Ace. (DOOR CLOSES) Well I'm happy to—who are *you?*

ACE: I'm Mr. Ace.

MONTEL: Oh you're the one who later became Mr. Ace.

ACE: What goes on here? Yes, I'm Mr. Ace—she couldn't make it today.

MONTEL: Oh no, oh no, I was hoping she would come. I've been on pins and cushions since she left here. I've been going besmerk.

ACE: Besmerk.

MONTEL: I've been trying to write a paper on her history—but my bearings are all bawled up.

ACE: Oh, brother.

MONTEL: Even my wife can't understand what's happened to me—and we've been insufferable companions for years.

ACE: Murder.

MONTEL: I've always been so fool face and fancy free—

ACE: Look, Ja—Doctor. I don't want my wife coming here any more. Will you please tell—

MONTEL: Not come here any more? She built the story up to the psycopathic moment and then she walked out. She's got to tell me what happened—you were in the car—you can tell me—you were speeding along in your car—*brbrbrbr*—the train was coming around the hill—*whoo whoo*—you couldn't stop—the train couldn't stop—what happened?

ACE: We were killed.

MONTEL: Oh *thank* you, Mr. Ace. Thank goodness. You took a load off my—you were killed?

ACE: Look, Doctor—

MONTEL: Interesting case. Lie down, Mr. Ace.

ACE: Me?

MONTEL: Very interesting. Now I want you to tell me the story of your life from as far back as you can remember.

ACE: Well I was born in a wild West show at the age of three—

MONTEL: Ah ha.

MUSIC BRIDGE

ACE: That doctor will never forget that hour, if he lives to be twelve years old. I fixed his wagon—because the very next day in his office—(FADE)

MONTEL: That's right—just lie back comfortably and relax. Now I want you to continue the story from where we left off:

TWO SPEECHES READ TOGETHER

JANE: Well, after we got out of the train wreck, the boy who later became Mr. Ace, my husband,

ACE: Well Doc, after I got out of the wild West show, I decided to become an Indian—

JANE: Dear, please—you're pushing me off the couch.

ACE: Well move over, Jane—I gotta have some room.

JANE: Move up a little—the palms of your feet are hanging over the end of the couch.

ACE: I can't move over—you push over a little.

JANE: I can't—there's no room.

ACE: Well, somebody's gotta move.

MOTHER: All right, children, if it makes you happy for me to move, I'll move.

MUSIC PLAYOFF

JANE FINDS A MATE FOR HER
MOTHER

ACE: Now we come to another program we did about your mother—remember we tried to get her married off, and you found this old widower?

JANE: Yes, and he was so funny. Who played that old man?

ACE: Art Carney. That was back in 1949 that we did this one.

JANE: In 1949—imagine—ten years ago.

ACE: That's the old math you're using. Actually 1949 was—

JANE: I don't care to hear it.

I should tell you before we get to this next script that around our house birthdays went out of style some years ago. One day at breakfast Jane said to me: "Well, dear, how do you feel this morning on your birthday?"

"Old," I replied.

"Now, dear, that's the wrong altitude."

"Well, Jane, I'm not exactly flying, if that's what you mean."

"No, I mean you keep forgetting what I told you. If I told you once, I told you twice. Don't say you're old, just say you're only getting older. Now repeat after me: I'm not old."

"I'm not old."

"I'm only getting older."

"I'm only getting older."

"Now, don't you feel better? You make it sound as if you're older than Macushla. From now on, we won't mention birthdays around here, if they upset you so. You are not old. You are only getting older. Right?"

"Right. But my glasses are old, and my ears."

"But not you. The word 'birthday' is tattoo around here."

And so with that indelibly inscribed, we haven't mentioned or celebrated our birthdays for some years. Although the day following that sparkling little chat I did find a package on the dresser. It was a sweater.

"I just happened to accidentally pass a store," she said, "and it was just your shade."

And it was. Sort of faded yellow. With a split infinitive. And that's how it's been—the day following every birthday she happens to accidentally pass a store, etc., etc.

That was about ten or twelve sweaters ago. Also, I confess to ten or twelve bottles of White Shoulders perfume from me. No parties, no cakes, no candles to blow out. Just accidentally passing stores through the leisurely flow of time.

And you want to know something? It has taken years off my age. The secret is simple. I pass it on to you. Follow carefully:

Since birthdays are not my bag any more, I haven't bothered to keep a chronological record. Some time ago, I had a birthday hiatus of three years. Then, I received a Hallmark thing from a sister. That reminded me of the date. So I simply added one year to the number at which I had left off three years before.

After four more years of no birthdays, there came a telegram to remind me. But I couldn't remember the number at which I had previously left off. So I selected an attractive, young number, and added one year to that. According to my abacus I am now a sexagenarian.

I like that word. It has a ring to it. A ring of excitement and elan. And, alas, of promise.

Jane didn't mention my birthday the next year. But there was this oblique reference: "I heard a funny joke today about age," she said. "I hope I can tell it right. Oh yes, I got it: A man is as old as he looks. A woman is as old as she likes. Ha, ha, ha."

"You heard that today?"

"Yes, don't you get it, dear?"

"That joke is not old. It's only getting older."

Now to read this script where Jane tried to shotgun her mother into marrying this old reprobate.

MUSIC: MANHATTAN SERENADE

ACE: *Ladies and gentlemen, Easy Aces.*

MUSIC OUT

ACE: It's the little things about Jane's mother that annoy me. For instance, I have a favorite easy chair I love to sit in after dinner. And in the four months she's been with us, Jane's mother had to pick that chair to sit in every night. I'll admit she does it fairly—she races me for it . . . And every time I pay two-eighty to place. Of course there are various ways I could get rid of my mother-in-law, and I'd have my chair back. I've thought 'em all over. First there's—

SOUND: TWO SHOTS

ACE: Then of course, there's—

SOUND: STRANGLING . . . BODY FALLS

ACE: Then there's a dandy—

SOUND: SPLASH OF WATER . . . GURGLING SOUND

ACE: I could get rid of her in any one of those ways, and I'd be sure to get the chair. But last week I hit upon a really diabolical scheme—and much safer. It began one night after dinner when we were in the living room. Jane was sitting at the desk writing a letter, I was standing in the middle of the room reading the evening paper, just for spite, and Mother was sitting in my easy chair, doodling.

MOTHER: (SINGS) Doodle, de do, doodle de do, doodle de do, doodle de do—

ACE: Mother—Mother—Mother, dear!

MOTHER: Yes?

ACE: (SOFTLY) Shut up!

JANE: Dear! Don't you lower your voice to my mother.

ACE: Jane, does she *have* to sit there in my chair, singing our song?

JANE: But dear, she's only doodling what comes naturally.

MOTHER: Please, Janie, don't argue on my account—after all this is his house; I'm only a stranger here. I never interfere with your privacy or comfort.

ACE: Smile when you say that, stranger.

JANE: Oh Mother, you know we want you to be happy. We can all be happy.

MOTHER: Happy. If it makes you happy to be happy, you be happy. Like your late father used to say, Janie—he was such a philosopher—he used to say, "What is happiness?" And I used to tell him, "Happiness is when your children grow up, and get married to a nice man who can take care of a poor mother in her declining years, and not make her feel she is a stranger and a burden, and look after her in sickness and in bad health—" that's what happiness is I used to tell your late father.

ACE: He was some philospher.

MOTHER: He used to say, "What is life?" And I used to tell him, "Life is when your children grow up, and get married to a nice man who can take care of a poor mother in her declining years—"

ACE: Jane, there's a basketball game tonight—I got two tickets —let's you and I go.

JANE: Basketball?

MOTHER: And when the children go out someplace they take the old mother with them—

ACE: It's a big national basketball tournament—the best teams in the country are there.

JANE: Oh, that sounds exciting.

MOTHER: Even an old mother would like a little excitement once in a while. After all it's only a matter of time till the old parents go upstairs to the Last Basketball Game of Them All.

ACE: Oh, *no*—

MOTHER: After all I've never seen a basketball game. Who knows if I'll even like it up there.

ACE: The only way to find out is to go up there and see.

JANE: But dear, you said you only got two tickets.

ACE: Yes, I've got two tickets—come on, Jane, get your coat and let's go.

JANE: But dear, we can't go off and leave m-o-t-h-e-r alone.

MOTHER: Oh don't worry about me, Janie—I'll get along. I'm not a child.

ACE: Sure she'll get along, Jane—let's go.

JANE: Will you be all right by yourself, Mother?

MOTHER: Oh, by myself, I'll be fine. If a burglar breaks into the house—well it doesn't matter. Of course it'll be a big shock—

ACE: He'll get over it—come on, Jane, let's go to the game.

JANE: Mother—will you promise to go to sleep early?

MOTHER: Sleep?—I haven't slept since I was eighteen years old. But it's all right. I'll make up some Ovaltine. I know how to light the gas stove, so if it explodes and blows up the house, I'll get to go out after all.

ACE: When you circle Madison Square Garden, buzz us.

JANE: Oh, Mother, you're always so pessimistic, why don't you be more of an optician.

MOTHER: Janie, I don't want you to worry. As soon as something happens, they'll notify you on the loudspeaker at the basketball game, between innings.

ACE: Yes, you're having your innings, all right.

MOTHER: You can always come down to the hospital and identify me. But if it's a close game, don't leave on my account. A few minutes won't make any difference—it'll be too late anyway. So go ahead—enjoy yourselves, have a good time.

ACE: All right, Jane, come on, let's go.

JANE: Oh dear, I *couldn't* go now. I'd never enjoy the game with Mother flying all over New York—I couldn't enjoy it, I don't care how many home runs we see.

ACE: All right—Look: here are two tickets—you and your mother go. I'll stay here.

MOTHER: Come on, Janie, get your coat—let's go.

JANE: But what about you, dear?

ACE: Oh I don't wanta be a bother, if I'm gonna be a bother, don't bother.

MOTHER: Come on, Janie—let's go.

JANE: But will you be all right here by yourself?

ACE: Oh, I'll be fine by myself. But if a gorgeous blonde walks in—oh well—

JANE: A blonde?

ACE: It's all right, Janie. They'll notify you between chuckers at the game and you can come down and identify me at the Copacabana . . . So enjoy yourself, have a good time.

MOTHER: Come on, Janie, let's go.

JANE: Oh, no. I wasn't born for nothing. Blondes, huh? Just wait till she gets here. I'll identify her. We're all staying home. (SILENCE)

ACE: Well I hope you're satisfied.

MOTHER: Me? What did I do?

ACE: Nothing. Nothing.

JANE: Well I guess I'll finish writing my letter.

ACE: Well, I'm gonna finish reading my paper . . . (PAUSE)

MOTHER: (SINGS) Doodle de do, doodle de do—doodle de do —doodle doo—

MUSIC BRIDGE

ACE: That was the night I reached the end of my rope . . . rope—say, I hadn't thought of that one. Naw, that's no good; besides she has no neck. But the next morning at the office was when I got that really clever, diabolical scheme. One of the fellows who works at the office with me—Charlie Harris—Charlie happened to drop in for a minute.

CHARLIE: What a basketball game last night, huh, Mr. Ace?

ACE: I understand it was.

CHARLIE: You understand it was? You had two seats for it.

ACE: Yes, I did. But I didn't go. How did you like the game?

CHARLIE: Well, as a matter of fact, I didn't go, either.

ACE: You had two tickets, didn't you?

CHARLIE: Yeh, but I couldn't make it last night. My wife's father is living with us now, and my wife didn't wanta leave him alone.

ACE: That's what happened with me. Only it's my wife's mother.

CHARLIE: We don't get to go any place since he came to live with us. He's a widower and—

ACE: Same thing at our house. She's a widow. We don't go any place since she came to live with us.

CHARLIE: What a bother!

ACE: Yeh—what a bother! . . . (PAUSE)

BOTH: Say, that's an idea . . . What were you about to say?
. . . No, no you go ahead.

ACE: Well I was only gonna say—

CHARLIE: Me too.

ACE: You mean?

CHARLIE: Why not?

ACE: How old is your father-in-law?

CHARLIE: He doesn't look a day over sixty. How old is your
mother-in-law?

ACE: Over fourteen.

CHARLIE: What?

ACE: I mean she's in great shape—spry as a colt, eats like a
horse.

CHARLIE: How tall is she?

ACE: Oh, about nineteen hands.

CHARLIE: Great—my father-in-law likes tall women.

ACE: Not that it matters, but is your father-in-law in good
shape?

CHARLIE: He's got a strong constitution.

ACE: Constitution—you should see my mother-in-law—skin
like parchment. You can see Guionette right on her
button.

CHARLIE: Well, what are we waiting for?

ACE: How about tonight?

CHARLIE: OK, he'll be there at eight o'clock if I have to wheel him over myself.

ACE: Great.

CHARLIE: Be sure your mother-in-law's there, and we'll put 'em both together.

ACE: You put your father-in-law together. By the time he gets there, I'll have my mother-in-law fully assembled.

CHARLIE: See you in church.

ACE: Yeh—

BOTH: (SING) Wedding March

MUSIC BRIDGE: MENDELSSOHN'S WEDDING MARCH

ACE: Well I had thought of everything else—drowning, strangling, hanging, but now I really had it: shotgun. I rushed home early from the office and told Jane the good news. Jane was tickled to death.

JANE: Hahah. Dear, stop tickling me.

ACE: Jane, this is it—we've solved the program. Eureka!

JANE: I do? It must be this new cologne I put on today—

ACE: Get your mother in here and let's talk her into it.

JANE: Mother married. Gee, I never thought of that. But it's a wonderful idea—I think every mother should be married.

ACE: Will you call her in? The guy is coming at eight o'clock.

JANE: What kind of a man is he?

ACE: A living man. What kind of a question is that? Call her in.

JANE: *Mother!*

MOTHER: (OFF) Yes, Janie.

JANE: *Mother can you come in here a minute?*

MOTHER: (OFF) I'll be right in, Janie.

ACE: Better let me tell her, Jane.

JANE: No dear, I wanta tell her. After all she's my mother, my own flesh and bones. (DOOR OPENS)

MOTHER: Did you wanta see me, Janie? There were some sparrows on the window sill in my room, I was going to feed them a little honey.

JANE: Come in, Mother, that's exactly what I wanted to talk to you about—about the birds and the bees.

ACE: Oh, *no*—tell her bluntly. Mother, you're having a gentleman caller tonight.

MOTHER: Gentleman caller?

ACE: Yes, he wants to get married.

MOTHER: If it makes him happy to get married, let him be happy.

JANE: But Mother, he wants to get married to you.

MOTHER: To me! Over my dead body.

ACE: Yes, we know.

JANE: Isn't it wonderful, Mother? We'll get you a new torso.

ACE: That I'd like to see.

JANE: After all, Mother, a woman is only young once in a while. Love makes the world go round together.

MOTHER: But, Janie, I don't even know him, much less love him.

JANE: Oh love—that comes later. Like when I got married. Remember, dear?

ACE: Jane—get to the point.

JANE: When we first got married we were in love, then we became friends, and now we're buddies.

ACE: Look, buddy—

MOTHER: But Janie, who is this man?

JANE: He's living. Isn't it exciting, Mother—can't you just smell the rice and old shoes?

MOTHER: That's a piece of liver I put on the stove for my dinner.

JANE: Oh Mother, can't you get interested in him—

MOTHER: Janie, when your late father was alive . . .

ACE: Look, Mother, let's don't go back to the past. Think of your future.

JANE: Yes, and think of the presents.

MOTHER: But a strange man, that I've never even met—I wouldn't even know how to go about it—it's been so long since I even looked at another man—

JANE: Mother, it's always the same. Love doesn't change. Because when two lovers woo, they still say I love you —you can rely on that—because as time goes by, moonlight and love songs are never out of date—hearts full of passion, jealousy and uh—

ACE: Hate.

JANE: Hate. Women needs man and man must have his mate, that no one can deny—it's still the same old story, a fight for—does this sound familiar to you, dear?

ACE: Play it again, Sam.

MUSIC BRIDGE: AS TIME GOES BY

ACE: Jane, of course, wasn't satisfied to let well enough alone, she had to play stup—cupid. That night while we were waiting for the old gentleman to come over, she started making with the counter plots. She was the captain in charge of the attack; zero hour had arrived. It was M-Day.

JANE: Mother—this is it. Gather around everybody—you too, dear.

ACE: Yes sir.

JANE: Everybody has a job to do, and if we pull together this'll be our clowning achievement. I don't want *any* slipups. Are you ready?

ACE: Synchronize your watches.

JANE: Mother, when he gets here, you be sitting on the couch, reading a book and smoking a cigarette with your legs crossed . . .

ACE: Neatest trick of the week.

JANE: And Mother, pull yourself in. Look slim. And as for you—

ACE: Sir, could I have a furlough?

JANE: After that big dinner?

ACE: Sorry, sir.

JANE: When he gets here, you'll wait till you get a signal from me, and you'll go up the corner drug store and telephone this number. And ask for Mother.

MOTHER: For me, Janie?

JANE: That's right Mother. He's gonna act like another man's calling you—and asking you for a date.

MOTHER: *Him?* He's not my type, Janie.

ACE: I'm not *your* type—

JANE: Please, Mother—after all, in order to get a man these days a girl's gotta play hard to take.

ACE: And she is.

JANE: By the time we finish with this man tonight, Mother, you'll be going steady with him.

MOTHER: Oh, Janie, the way I shake all the time, how can I go steady?

JANE: So when he goes to the corner and calls you up, this man'll see that a lot of men are trying to take you out—that you're not a wallpaper— (DOOR BELL RINGS)

ACE: There he is—this is it—everybody into their fox holes. I'll let him in.

JANE: OK, sit down, Mother—take the book—sit up straight—chins up—that's it.

MOTHER: Janie, you're making me so nervous. (DOOR OPENS)

ACE: (OFF) How do you do, sir.

WILSON: (OFF) How do you do—Mrs. Sherwood live here?

ACE: (OFF) That's right. Come in, come in— (DOOR CLOSES) I'm Mr. Ace.

WILSON: (OFF) (COUGHS LOUD AND LONG) I'm Georgie Wilson.

ACE: Georgie? Yes, come in, son. May I take your coat?

WILSON: (COUGH) No, gotta keep it on for a few minutes till I get used to the temperature in here. (BIG LONG COUGH)

ACE: That's quite a cough you got there, Mr. Wilson.

WILSON: You like it? You should have heard it yesterday— it was a piperoo. Came from way down here in my bronchal tubes. Doctor gave me some medicine and all I got left now is a post-nasal drip.

ACE: Yes. Well come on in. I want you to meet my wife. This is Mr. Wilson, Jane.

JANE: Please to meet your acquaintance.

WILSON: (COUGHS) Howdy-do.

JANE: And you may think this is my sister, Mr. Wilson, but she's really my mother.

MOTHER: (GIGGLES) How do you do, Mr. Wilson.

WILSON: (COUGHS) Howdy do, Mrs. Sherwood. Here—I brung you a tin of chocolates—

MOTHER: Well, thank you.

WILSON: Not at all, not at all—you'll find they're gentle and fast acting. Take 'em regularly myself.

MOTHER: My favorite brand.

JANE: Won't you sit down, Mr. Wilson? On this couch over here—

WILSON: No, thanks, gotta sit on a hard chair. Sacroilliac, you know.

MOTHER: Sacroilliac—why I got that too.

JANE: Well, you two have a lot that's common.

WILSON: Oh that ain't half of what I got. I got a blood pressure of 180.

MOTHER: A hundred and eighty—at its lowest mine's 190.

WILSON: I got neuritis in every one of my ten fingers.

MOTHER: I got neuritis in nine fingers, and in my tenth finger I got bursitis . . .

WILSON: (COUGH) Hear that cough? How do you like that cough? (COUGH)

MOTHER: It's fair.

WILSON: Fair! Comes from way down in my lungs.

MOTHER: Lungs. Who's got lungs?

WILSON: I got a silver plate in my head.

MOTHER: I got service for six. . . . (PAUSE)

WILSON: (COUGHS) Well, five years ago I died.

ACE: Top that, Mother.

WILSON: Haha—I was gone for ten minutes.

MOTHER: Really? Sit over by me, Georgie.

JANE: Dear, how about some cigars?

ACE: I'm sorry, I'm all out of 'em. Would you like a cigarette?

JANE: No, dear, cigar store.

ACE: Oh yes—cigar store . . . excuse me—I'll be right back. (DOOR OPENS AND CLOSES)

JANE: Well, Mr. Wilson—can I get you something?

WILSON: Yes you can. Get me some bicarbonate. Always take a spoonful of bicarbonate after dinner.

MOTHER: I always take two spoonfuls.

WILSON: I used to take a heaping tablespoonful.

JANE: Well, I guess I better go if you two are gonna sit here spooning.

WILSON: (COUGHS)

MOTHER: What are you taking for that cough, Georgie?

WILSON: Pretty good one, isn't it?

MOTHER: I got a wonderful home remedy cough. My mother used it till the day she died. And my brother, rest his soul, swore by it. And an uncle of mine used it all the time and never had a sick day in his life, may he rest in peace. But my stubborn old grandmother wouldn't use it at all—and she suffered all through her ninety-five years. (PHONE RINGS)

JANE: Oh. Is that the telephone? Don't move, kids, I'll answer it. I'm in again. (PHONE UP) Hello.

ACE: (FILTER) Hello, Jane, I didn't go to the cigar store. I'm calling from the phone down in the lobby.

JANE: Oh yes, she is—uh—Gregory—but she's busy. I'll see if she can talk. Mother, it's for you.

MOTHER: For me? Who is it?

JANE: Oh I don't know—one of your boy friends. Honestly, Mr. Wilson, she's got more friends than she knows how.

WILSON: (COUGHS)

MOTHER: I can't talk to him, Janie—I'm busy.

JANE: Hello, she says she can't talk to you, Gregory—she's busy.

ACE: Oh that's a shame—I was gonna take her out to dinner tonight.

JANE: Well, some other night.

ACE: But I got two tickets to the wax museum.

JANE: You mean the theater—

ACE: Jane, do I have to keep this up?

JANE: Haha, yes you do.

ACE: Well, all right, I got two tickets to the theater—and after that reservations at the Stork Club.

JANE: Stork Club?

ACE: And then I thought we'd drop in at the Copacabana— got a hot rumba band there.

JANE: Rumba band—yes—

ACE: And maybe stop in at Twenty-One for a late snack— wonderful food there—pretty expensive, but I don't care.

JANE: You don't? Well, Mother can't make it—but I can. I'll be down in a few minutes. Wait for me.

ACE: Oh no, Jane—what are you doing?

MUSIC BRIDGE

ACE: Getting Jane's mother married off, turned out to be quite a project. It wasn't exactly love at first sight, because neither she nor Mr. Wilson could see. After all this wasn't exactly adolescent love, it was more *con*valescent love. In a week, though, Mother was wearing his picture in her locket—it was an X-ray . . . he has a beautiful appendix. I was quite happy about the thing, but one night, I awoke to find Jane pacing the floor—

JANE: Dear, do you know it's nearly one o'clock, and they're not back yet.

ACE: So what?

JANE: So what? Oh where are our parents tonight?

ACE: They went to a movie—and probably stopped to have a bite at a restaurant.

JANE: Are these our Child's?

ACE: Oh, stop, Jane—you're getting hysterical.

JANE: That's the thanks you get from parents—staying out till all hours of the night—worrying their children—some times I don't think it's worth having them.

ACE: Jane, they're just in a restaurant. Aren't you getting a little excited over nothing? Come back to sleep.

JANE: Sleep. I've been sound awake all night. Turning and tossing—first heads, then tails. I've gotta have a talk with Mother.

ACE: Man to man. (SOUND OF KEY IN DOOR AND DOOR OPENS AND CLOSES)

JANE: Yes.

ACE: Look, I don't think—

JANE: Oh here she is—is that you, Mother?

MOTHER: (OFF) Yes, Janie.

JANE: Well it's about time you got home—where have you been?

MOTHER: Georgie and I went to the theater.

JANE: Theater—what theater stays open so late?

MOTHER: The amphitheater over at the hospital.

ACE: Oh, great . . .

JANE: What theater did she say—I didn't get it—

ACE: She's been over at the hospital sitting in the amphitheater watching the doctors operate.

MOTHER: They had a double feature tonight: appendix and tonsillitis.

ACE: No shorts?

MOTHER: Well they did shorten one fellow's nose but that wasn't very exciting.

JANE: Doesn't he ever take you to any movies?

MOTHER: Well, we went once, but you see Georgie can't hear well and he has to sit up close—and of course I'm farsighted and I have to sit way back—and it gets very tiresome running up and down the aisle to hold hands.

JANE: Mother, we have to have a talk.

ACE: Not now, Jane, it's late. Let's go to sleep.

JANE: I can't sleep until I find out what's going on here. Mother, has Mr. Wilson said anything about his intentions?

MOTHER: What do you mean intentions, Janie?

JANE: Mother, do I have to draw a bluepoint for you?

ACE: Yes, mother, don't clam up.

JANE: Dear, let me handle this. Mother, maybe you're satisfied to run around like this helter shelter every night—but not me. After all Mother, it's time you settle down. Hasn't Mr. Wilson said anything about getting . . . shall-we-say married?

ACE: Yes, let's say that.

JANE: Dear, please, stay out of this. Are you my mother's keeper?

ACE: Yes. Now, Mother, why don't you go to your cage—room—

JANE: Well, Mother—what about it? Has Mr. Wilson said anything?

MOTHER: Well nothing definite—unless you can call this ring definite.

JANE: Ring—did he give you a ring?

MOTHER: Here it is—you can see for yourself.

JANE: Oh what a beautiful ring.

MOTHER: It's a genuine fourteen-karat gallstone.

ACE: No kidneying—let me see it.

MUSIC BRIDGE

ACE: Well, everybody, the drinks are on me—looks like it's all set—you know the old saying—something old, something old—something borrowed, something blew. That was my top: I just blew it. Have another drink—oh go ahead—here take a handful of rice to throw at the bride— oh no, don't touch those old shoes—I wanta throw those myself—they're my old baseball shoes with the spikes— How am I so sure they're gonna get married? Well, the other night after dinner, Jane dashed into the living room with a big secret.

JANE: Dear—guess what Mother's doing.

ACE: Reading her book, *Arthritis Can Be Fun?*

JANE: No—she's packing her suitcase.

ACE: Packing a sui—no kidding—how do you know?

JANE: I was just eavesdripping. You know what this *means*, dear?

ACE: They're gonna elope?

JANE: If I'm wrong, I'm not far from it . . . A runaway marriage—well, like daughter like mother!

ACE: What are you talking about?

JANE: Oh, you know when you used to call on me, every time Mother mentioned marriage you'd run away.

ACE: Like daughter like mother. Well they're finally gonna do it. Isn't it wonderful?

JANE: (CRYING) Yes, dear, it's wonderful.

ACE: Oh now, Jane, stop crying—

JANE: Oh I know I shouldn't, dear. I keep saying to myself— It's not losing a mother but gaining a son-in-law.

ACE: Son-in-law—Jane, old man Wilson isn't—Jane, the phone—

JANE: I was just going to. Hello—

CHARLIE: (FILTER) Is that you, Jane? This is Charlie.

JANE: Just fine.

CHARLIE: Guess what's going on here? The old man's packing his suitcase.

JANE: Yes I just saw her—Oh, you mean Mr. Wilson?

ACE: What is it, Jane?

JANE: Mr. Wilson is packing a suitcase too.

ACE: Oh that's wonderful—let me talk to him.

JANE: But not loud—we don't want them to know they're going to elope.

ACE: Hello, Charlie, Jane's mother is packing a suitcase too.

CHARLIE: Yeh, I just heard.

ACE: Isn't that wonderful. It's all so sudden.

CHARLIE: Sudden. For years the old man has been walking around with a marriage license made out to whom it may concern.

ACE: Look, Charlie, you better get out of the house, and so will we, so they can elope without an audience.

CHARLIE: OK, "brother." So long.

ACE: Haha OK, "brother." So long. (HANGS UP) Come on, Jane, let's go to a movie or something.

JANE: OK, dear—oh I better tell Mother we're going. But,

listen, not a word to her that we know about the elopement.

ACE: I won't. Just make sure you don't spill it.

JANE: Me? You know me, dear.

ACE: That's what I mean.

JANE: *Mother.*

MOTHER: (OFF) *Yes, Janie, what is it?*

JANE: *Mother we're going out to a movie, will you be all right by yourself?*

MOTHER: *Oh, I'll be fine. Have a nice time.*

JANE: *We will.* Say good night, dear.

ACE: *Good night, Mother.*

MOTHER: *Good night, son.*

JANE: Aw, isn't that sweet—she called you son. *Good night Mother.*

MOTHER: *Good night Janie.*

ACE: That's enough, Jane—come on let's go.

JANE: *We'll see you when we get back from the movies.*

MOTHER: *All right, Janie, but don't wait up for me.*

JANE: *We won't, Mother.*

ACE: That's enough Jane—come on.

JANE: *Good night, Mother, may all your troubles be little ones.*

ACE: Oh *no,* Jane—isn't that awful?

MUSIC BRIDGE

ACE: Well the next three days were sheer heaven—with a maraschino cherry on top. I lolled around in my favorite chair to my heart's content. We were both extremely happy. Except Jane. She missed her mother, I guess— and, if the truth were known, I had a pang or two myself. You can get so used to something, you know—that fragrance of fresh iodine she used to exude . . . Then one night—suddenly—and without warning—the door opened —and there they stood—the bag—and Mother.

JANE: Mother!

MOTHER: Hello, Janie.

ACE: Mother—you're not alone?

JANE: Yes, Mother where's your husband?

MOTHER: Husband!

ACE: Where's Mr. Wilson?

JANE: Mother, didn't you get married?

MOTHER: Married. Why Janie, I've only known the man a week or two. Maybe some day, but—

ACE: But where did you go—with that suitcase—

JANE: Mother, never darken my doorstep again.

MOTHER: Janie, you misunderstand. Don't you remember I told you we've been going to the amphitheater.

ACE: Don't tell me you two have been spending the weekend watching operations?

MOTHER: Oh no—we got into the act this time.

ACE: Into the act?

MOTHER: Yes, Georgie's been bothered with that post-nasal

drip—so he had an operation performed on his nose. And I had an operation performed too.

JANE: Mother—you had an operation. Where?

MOTHER: Well, Janie, you know where I told you it's been bothering me lately?

JANE: You had it operated on?

MOTHER: That's right, Janie.

JANE: Dear—get up and let mother sit in that easy chair.

ACE: Well, this is where I came in.

MUSIC—PLAYOFF

EPILOGUE

"Well, Jane, that ought to be enough scripts for a book. What do you think?"

"I think this is the picture of both of us I'd like to use. Remember when we took this?"

"Vaguely. If you ask me I think all these photographs that were taken back in the thirties and forties aren't right for this book. Whom are we kidding? Now here's one—it was taken about a month ago."

"No sir!"

"She said emphatically. What's the matter with it? It's our latest picture."

"It's *too* late."

"Too late? Oh come on, Jane, you look as lovely in this picture as you ever did."

"You do? Well, if you say so. But they just don't make cameras like they used to years ago, do they, dear?"